NEW BROOCHES
400+ CONTEMPORARY JEWELLERY DESIGNS

BROCHES
400+ DISEÑOS DE JOYERÍA CONTEMPORÁNEA

NICOLAS ESTRADA

HOAKI

HOAKI

Hoaki Books, S.L.
C/ Ausiàs March, 128
08013 Barcelona, Spain
T. 0034 935 952 283
F. 0034 932 654 883
info@hoaki.com
www.hoaki.com

hoakibooks

Contemporary Art Jewellery
New Brooches. 400+ Contemporary Jewellery Designs
Broches. 400+ Diseños de joyería contemporánea

ISBN English: 978-84-17656-94-2
ISBN Spanish: 978-84-19220-10-3

Second edition: 2022

© 2022 Hoaki Books, S.L.

Selection of contents and edition: Nicolas Estrada
English translation and revision: Tom Corkett
Spanish translation and revision: Montse Borràs
Layout: Vasilisa Aristarkhova
Image correction: Alicia Martorell
Editorial coordination: Montse Borràs
Introductory texts by:
© Ezra Satok – Wolman
© Ramón Puig Cuyàs
© Nicolas Estrada

D.L. English: B 12687-2022
D.L. Spanish: B 12688-2022

Printed in China

PREFACE BY THE AUTHOR

Nicolas Estrada

This book would not have been so beautiful and valuable had it not been for the extraordinary response from jewellers to my call for submissions, and so I want to express my sincere thanks to all the people who trusted my ideas and sent in contributions, which gave me the opportunity – and the real privilege – to see jewellery pieces from around the world by artists of exceptional talent.

I had the immense pleasure of receiving and reviewing 1,360 contributions, from which 172 participants were finally chosen. Selecting the best images was a tough job, and I knew that I would have to set aside many good offerings. And so I would like to set out the criteria that were applied to select the images contained in this book.

Having published five books about the jewellery world, there are three things that I greatly appreciate: the fact that participants take the time to read, understand and respect the terms of the call for contributions; applications that are received in a timely manner; and extraordinary and wonderful applications in which everything fits together perfectly. Applications that arrive in good time allow me to work deliberately and to establish a satisfactory and rewarding dialogue with the participant. Everything works smoothly when the photographs provided perfectly explain the pieces and when they arrive in the required format and through the specified channels. These are the kinds of applications that define the structure of the book. Around 70% of the proposals reached me just before the deadline for entries. During the final days, things move at a dizzying and almost frantic pace, and there is hardly any time left to establish a of dialogue with the participants.

In the second month after the call for submissions had been made, I realized that I had come up against a major obstacle: How could I show jewellery lovers that all these wonderful objects were actually brooches? I was struck by the worshipful way in which jewellers can treat their creations. There were brooches that were conceived as collection pieces or works of art, and jewellery pieces that were designed to adorn the displays of galleries or walls of museums. They were photographed in a two-dimensional way, as though they were paintings. The wearer was completely pushed aside: these were pieces designed to be exhibited, not worn. At this point, I started to select pieces where one could tell that the wonderful objects on display were actually brooches, either because the photos of them showed them on the body, or because it was possible to spot their pins, that simple element so representative of brooches. And yes, the selection process was very complex – so much so that I have to admit that no place could be found for many pieces of remarkable beauty and personality on these pages.

I have always worked alone. At times, I have told myself that for my next book I'll find someone to help me. But I never do. My own work and research directions have led me to appreciate working individually to the highest degree, as my deep commitment to such a demanding challenge prevents me from delegating duties.

The two introductory texts that open this book – The Brooch by Ramón Puig Cuyàs and A Brooch Is Not Simply A Brooch by Ezra Satok-Wolman – lend it a beauty and a sensitivity. I would like to offer my sincerest thanks to both Ramón and Ezra for contributing their talent and experience to this wonderful visual journey.

Ramón was my teacher at the Escola Massana in the mid-2000s. It was through his hands that I came to learn about artistic jewellery, and I fell in love with this profession in his classes. For this reason, it is a great honour that the person who opened the doors to this incredible world to me agreed to open the amazing collection contained in this book. Thank you, Ramón.

I met Ezra thanks to Klimt02, and through a series of articles on the identity crisis in jewellery that he published in 2014. Those articles led me to write to him, and we exchanged a series of emails. We met in person during Genesis, his first exhibition in Barcelona. His decision to write another of the texts in this book is a great honour for me. Thank you, Ezra.

I would also like to thank Promopress, the publisher that trusted in my judgement and that allowed me to share jewellery that, although wonderful, is still unfamiliar to many. I would like to thank very especially Joaquim Canet and Montse Borràs for all the help that they provided me with, and my thanks also go to the team of professionals tasked with making this book as beautiful as the works that it contains and with making these works known and admired all over the world.

New Brooches features 172 participants, 441 photos, 566 brooches, five chapters and two texts. I hope that each of you enjoys each and every page and is able to appreciate the great effort that lies behind a publication such as this one. Many thanks!

PREFACIO DEL AUTOR

Nicolas Estrada

Este libro no sería tan bello y valioso sin la extraordinaria acogida que tuvo la convocatoria, por eso quiero manifestar mi más sincero agradecimiento a todas las personas que confiaron en mi criterio y enviaron su solicitud, lo que me ha permitido la oportunidad de ver piezas realizadas en casi todo el mundo por artistas de talento excepcional; todo un privilegio.

Tuve el inmenso placer de recibir y examinar 1.360 para finalmente elegir a 172 participantes. Fue un trabajo muy arduo seleccionar las mejores imágenes sabiendo que debería dejar de lado tan buen material, por eso quiero sustentar claramente cuál fue el criterio de selección de las imágenes que contiene este libro.

Después de haber publicado cinco libros sobre el universo de la joyería, hay tres cosas que agradezco inmensamente: el hecho de que los participantes se tomen el tiempo para leer, entender y respetar las bases de la convocatoria, las solicitudes recibidas con antelación, y las solicitudes extraordinarias y maravillosas en las que todo encaja perfectamente. Las solicitudes que llegan con tiempo me permiten trabajar pausadamente y establecer un diálogo satisfactorio y enriquecedor con el participante. Todo fluye cuando las fotografías explican las piezas a la perfección, los textos llegan completos, en el formato requerido y a través de los programas sugeridos; estas son las solicitudes que finalmente definen la estructura del libro. Cerca del 70% de las solicitudes me llegan al final del período de convocatoria y durante los últimos cinco días la actividad es de un ritmo vertiginoso y casi frenético, sin tiempo de entablar ningún tipo de diálogo con el participante.

Durante el segundo mes de la convocatoria me di cuenta de que me enfrentaba a un obstáculo importante: ¿cómo mostrar a los amantes de la joyería que todos estos objetos maravillosos eran en realidad broches? Me impactó el culto que muchos de los joyeros rinden a sus creaciones, el broche como objeto de colección, como pieza de arte, joyas concebidas para adornar la vitrina de una galería o la pared de un museo, fotografiadas bidimensionalmente, como una pintura, en las que el portador queda totalmente relegado: joyas concebidas para ser expuestas, no para ser llevadas. Fue entonces cuando empecé a seleccionar las piezas en las que se veía que esos objetos maravillosos eran en realidad broches, bien fuese porque la fotografía los enseñaba en el cuerpo o porque en ella se lograba identificar una aguja, ese elemento tan simple y representativo de los broches. Y sí, fue una selección muy difícil, tanto así que debo reconocer que muchas piezas de notable belleza y personalidad no encontraron su lugar en estas páginas.

Siempre he trabajado solo, a menudo he dicho que para el próximo libro conseguiré a una persona que me asista, pero nunca lo hago; mi propia labor y mis caminos de investigación me han llevado a saber apreciar en grado sumo el hecho de poder trabajar individualmente, pues mi profundo compromiso con un evento tan exigente me impide delegar responsabilidades.

Los dos textos introductorios que abren el libro aportan belleza y sensibilidad a la publicación: El Broche de Ramón Puig Cuyàs y Un broche no es tan solo un broche de Ezra Satok-Wolman. A ambos, mi más sincero agradecimiento por contribuir con su talento y experiencia a este maravilloso recorrido visual.

Ramón fue mi profesor en la Escola Massana a mediados de 2000. De su mano conocí la joyería artística y en sus clases me enamoré de esta profesión. Por eso es un gran honor que quien me abrió las puertas a este increíble mundo haya accedido a abrir este maravilloso recorrido. Muchas gracias, Ramón.

Conocí a Ezra gracias a Klimt02 a través de una serie de artículos sobre la crisis de identidad en la joyería, que publicó en el 2014 y que me condujeron a escribirle y cruzar una serie de correos electrónicos. Después nos conocimos personalmente durante Genesis, su primera exposición en Barcelona. Es un gran honor para mí que haya aceptado escribir otro de los textos de este libro. Muchas gracias, Ezra.

Y a Promopress, editorial que me plantea la publicación de estos libros, agradezco que siga confiando en mi criterio y permitiéndome exponer toda esta joyería que, aunque maravillosa, es todavía desconocida para tantos. Muy especialmente, agradezco a Joaquim Canet y a Montse Borràs toda la ayuda que me brindan y a un equipo de profesionales que se encargan de que este libro sea tan precioso como los trabajos que incluye y de que sea conocido y admirado por todo el mundo.

Este libro incluye 172 participantes, 441 fotos, 566 broches, cinco capítulos y dos textos. Espero que cada uno de ustedes disfrute de sus páginas y logre apreciar el gran esfuerzo que hay detrás de una publicación como esta. ¡Muchísimas gracias!

NEW BROOCHES

Ramón Puig Cuyàs

In primitive times, an ornament placed on the body was more than a sign. It was an act of magic, whose main purpose was protection – a defence against the wild and the hostile. It was a way to exorcise fear of the uncontrollable and unknown outside world. Body ornamentation was a symbolic code that allowed primitive man to represent himself and communicate with the invisible and transcendental world. It was a way of defining his spiritual identity, and it helped him to better understand and control the forces within his magical universe.

There were three fundamental types of symbolic ornamentation: permanent tattoos, more ephemeral body painting, and objects that were placed on the body and mainly hung around the neck and also the limbs.

However, geographical and climate conditions restricted use of the first two types of ornamentation to warm climates where it was not necessary to cover the body in order to protect it from inclement weather. In the north's humid and cold climates, skins and fabrics covered most of the body, and therefore objects placed on it had greater importance. These included necklaces and bracelets, and later on torques, earrings, rings, medallions, clips placed directly on the clothing, and buckles and fasteners for belts, fibulae and so forth. The brooch's ancestor is the fibula, which appeared in the Bronze age and was used for millennia through the various cultures. The fibula primarily had the practical function of holding and adjusting the pieces of cloth that covered the body. It is a needle with a safety mechanism – like a safety pin – and it evolved into a variety of shapes and decorations, from the simplest iron or bronze pieces to ones finely crafted from silver and gold. It had an eminently practical function, but it was also used as a symbol of social status and wealth.

Gradually the fibula, a word that comes from the Greek for needle, became a brooch. The brooch's symbolic function prevailed over its practical role, and it would affix to itself over the top of the clothing. It is composed of two parts: a back where the needle is attached, and a front that contains the decorative motifs. It emerged gradually, becoming increasingly used from the Middle Ages onward. This coincided with the increasingly widespread use of the button, though forerunners to the button existed from 2000 BC. The brooch gained increasing prominence as a clothing accessory through the Renaissance, Mannerism, the Baroque and the Rococo, and it took centre stage in the nineteenth century.

In today's Western societies, the brooch is not one of the most frequently used kinds of jewellery in everyday life, but it is the most important. With the exception of the creations of high-jewellery makers, earrings, rings, necklaces, bracelets and small pendants are commonly used by the majority of ordinary people as a more or less discreet clothing and fashion accessory. However, perhaps because of its frontal visibility, the brooch has maintained its importance as a symbolic element and as an amplifier of the user's identity. It is used for special and socially relevant occasions. The best-known case is that of the former United States Secretary of State, Madeleine Albright, who had a whole arsenal of brooches and used them as a way to send visual messages to her political partners, combining them according to whether she was meeting with allies or adversaries.

The brooch works differently to most other types of jewellery. For example, earrings can be covered up by the hair, and necklaces, chains and bracelets can be partially hidden by/ clothing. Moreover, these types of jewellery rest against the skin and are in direct contact with the body. The brooch is fastened to clothing and remains at a distance from the body. This gives the brooch a more formal freedom, as it is not so subject to the shape of the body or to ergonomic factors.

Brooches say a lot about their wearers. The brooch faces forward and outward, and this frontal nature increases its symbolic function and gives it surprising expressive power. The brooch helps to construct an important part of the public personality that we want to display, but it can also express our inner and more intimate world.

Some artists such as Peter Skubic and Antón Cepka have expressed the idea that the brooch can function as a small sculpture on a dress or jacket. At other times, it may be seen as a two-dimensional form, like a low-relief piece or a small painting, but it always has high interpersonal communicative value. Perhaps for these reasons, the brooch is one of the most widely used types of jewellery in contemporary artistic jewellery. For an artist, the brooch offers a freedom of expression that is not found in other, perhaps more decorative forms of jewellery.

This type of piece is usually associated with women wearers, but in a society that is tending toward eliminating gender differences, the brooch is perhaps the most widely accepted type of jewellery to be worn both by women and by men. There are many men who buy and collect brooches in order to wear them.

When a brooch is a little work of art, it takes on a special dimension and allows us to share the values of contemporary art in our daily relationships with the people close to us.

EL BROCHE

Ramón Puig Cuyàs

En las primeras culturas, el ornamento primitivo sobrepuesto al cuerpo, más que un signo, era un acto mágico, cuya principal finalidad era la defensa contra una naturaleza salvaje y hostil. Era una forma de exorcizar el miedo hacia el mundo exterior, incontrolable y desconocido. La ornamentación corporal era un código simbólico que permitía al hombre primitivo representarse y comunicarse con el mundo invisible y trascendental. Definir su identidad espiritual le ayudaba a comprender mejor y controlar las fuerzas de su universo mágico.

Había tres tipos fundamentales de ornamentación simbólica: el tatuaje, de carácter permanente, la pintura corporal, con un carácter más efímero y los objetos sobrepuestos al cuerpo, que fundamentalmente se cuelgan del cuello y también en las extremidades. Pero la climatología restringe la práctica de las dos primeras tipologías ornamentales a climas cálidos, donde no es necesario cubrir el cuerpo para protegerlo de las inclemencias del tiempo. En los climas húmedos y fríos del norte, las pieles y los tejidos cubren la mayor parte del cuerpo y por lo tanto tienen mayor importancia los objetos sobrepuestos al cuerpo: collares, brazaletes, y más tarde torques, pendientes, anillos, medallones prendidos directamente sobre la vestimenta, hebillas o cierres para cinturones, fíbulas, etc. El antepasado del broche es la fíbula, que aparece en la edad del bronce y que se usará durante milenios en diversas culturas. La fíbula tenía la función práctica de sujetar y ajustar las piezas de tela con los que se cubrían el cuerpo. Consistía en una aguja con un mecanismo de seguridad, como un imperdible, y evolucionó en una gran variedad de formas y decoraciones, desde las más sencillas en hierro o bronce, a las finamente trabajadas en plata y oro, por lo que también se usaron como símbolo de estatus social y de riqueza.

La fíbula, que proviene de la palabra griega que significaba aguja, se transformó paulatinamente en broche, cuya función fue más simbólica. Está compuesto por la parte trasera, en la que se sujeta la aguja, y la parte delantera, con los motivos decorativos. Su aparición fue gradual, siendo cada vez mas usados a partir de la baja Edad Media, coincidiendo con el uso cada vez mas generalizado del botón, aunque ya existían antecedentes del botón desde el siglo XX a.C. El broche irá teniendo cada vez mas protagonismo como complemento del vestir y la moda a través del Renacimiento, el Manierismo, el Barroco, el Rococó, y alcanzando pleno protagonismo social durante el siglo XIX.

En la actualidad el broche no es la joya más utiliza en la vida cotidiana, pero sí el más importante. Si exceptuamos las creaciones de las firmas de alta joyería, los pendientes, anillos, collares, pulseras y pequeños colgantes son habitualmente utilizados como un complemento mas o menos discreto del vestir. Pero el broche, quizás por su visibilidad frontal, conserva su importancia como elemento simbólico, que refleja la identidad del usuario. Se utiliza para ocasiones especiales y de relevancia social. El caso mas conocido es el de la ex Secretaria de Estado de los Estados Unidos, Madeleine Albraight, que poseía todo un arsenal de broches que utilizaba como una forma de enviar mensajes visuales a sus interlocutores políticos, combinándolos según se entrevistara con aliados o adversarios.

El broche funciona de manera diferente a la mayoría de otros tipos de joyas, como los pendientes que pueden quedar tapados por el pelo, o los collares, cadenas y pulseras que pueden quedar semiocultos por la ropa. Además, estas joyas se apoyan sobre la piel y están en contacto directo con el cuerpo. El broche se sujeta sobre el vestido y se distancia del cuerpo, y por ello queda más libre de las formas del cuerpo y los condicionantes ergonómicos.

El broche revela mucho de su usuario; mira hacia fuera, y esta naturaleza frontal potencia su función simbólica y le confiere un sorprendente poder expresivo. El broche contribuye a construir la personalidad que queremos mostrar, pero también puede expresar nuestro mundo interior y más intimo.

Algunos artistas, como Peter Skubic o Antón Cepka, han expresado la idea de que el broche puede funcionar como una pequeña escultura prendida del vestido o de la chaqueta. En otras ocasiones puede verse como una forma más bidimensional, como un bajo relieve o una pequeña pintura, pero siempre presenta un alto valor comunicativo interpersonal.

Quizás por estas razones el broche es una de las tipologías más utilizadas por la joyera artística contemporánea, pues proporciona una libertad de expresión que no se da en otras formas de joyería, quizás más decorativas.
En general la joya se entiende como un objeto de uso mayoritariamente femenino, pero en una sociedad que tiende a eliminar las diferencias de género, el broche es quizás el tipo de joya más aceptado para ser llevado indistintamente por hombres y mujeres. Muchos hombres compran y coleccionan broches para poder llevarlos.

Cuando el broche se convierte en una pequeña obra de arte, adquiere una dimensión extraordinaria y permite compartir los valores del arte contemporáneo cotidianamente con las personas que tenemos cerca.

Ezra Satok-Wolman | p. 176

A BROOCH IS NOT SIMPLY A BROOCH

Ezra Satok-Wolman

I have always been a big fan of brooches, so I was quite flattered when I was approached to write a short essay on the topic for this book. In preparing to do so I began to consider what it is about the brooch that makes it so appealing to me both as a jewellery maker and as a collector of contemporary jewellery. This is something that I have previously given thought to, but I needed to explore it further in order to put my thoughts into words. From the perspective of the jewellery maker the brooch allows for a certain amount of freedom in design and creative potential that is unparalleled by other types of jewellery. As a vehicle for creative concepts, the brooch allows the maker to involve a level of depth that can result in something truly spectacular.

The brooch is very unique when compared to rings, necklaces and earrings. I regard the brooch as both object and as jewellery, tending not to prioritize one over the other. In that sense the brooch presents a beautiful duality that I don't necessarily see with other types of jewellery, or at least not in the same way. The brooch seems to have a raison d'être with or without interaction with the body, whereas other types of jewellery seem to be missing something when the human element is not present. Perhaps this can be attributed in part to the brooch not physically interacting with the body and therefore not requiring the body to empower the object.

Brooches tend to have a certain amount of neutrality which has always appealed to me. When I am creating a brooch I never consciously think about whether the piece is intended for a man or a woman. My focus is always on creating the piece. Brooches tend to blur the lines of gender and appeal to people based on their personal taste rather than whether the piece is suited for one gender or another. Perhaps this is again a byproduct of the brooch not physically interacting with the wearer directly – therefore the body not being overly important in the process of design or creation. It could also be related to the idea that the brooch exists, regardless of whether it is being worn or not.

One of the biggest challenges a jewellery artist faces is integrating a creative concept into a wearable object without having to compromise too much of the initial idea in doing so. Many types of jewellery present design challenges or restrictions that relate to how the piece of jewellery will fit or feel. Ultimately elements of the initial idea may be compromised in exchange for functionality or wearability, but this rarely impacts the design of a brooch due to the very simple requirements that constitute functionality. Needing only a pin to secure a brooch to the wearer's garment, the brooch is essentially a jewellery artist's blank canvas, so long as it meets that single requirement.

The versatile and dynamic nature of the brooch is evident throughout the entire spectrum of jewellery. Brooches are made in an infinite number of materials, using an infinite number of techniques and possess all the best qualities of sculpture, architecture and painting, scaled down to an intimate and personal size. Brooches comment on social and political themes and values, philosophical ideas, personal experiences and explore geometric or abstract forms. The brooch has continued to evolve and be reinterpreted by hand and machine, playing a critical role in the development of new jewellery as a platform for artistic expression. There has been no better time than the present to explore and document this subject.

Ezra Satok-Wolman | p. 176

UN BROCHE NO ES TAN SOLO UN BROCHE

Ezra Satok-Wolman

Siempre me han encantado los broches, por esa razón me sentí muy halagado cuando me propusieron escribir un pequeño texto de introducción sobre el tema para abrir este libro. Mientras me preparaba, empecé a pensar qué hace que los broches me resulten tan atractivos, como joyero pero también como coleccionista. Es algo en lo que ya he pensado en otras ocasiones, pero quería explorar en profundidad el tema para poder volcar mis pensamientos en palabras. Desde la perspectiva del joyero, el broche proporciona una cierta libertad en el diseño y sus posibilidades creativas van más allá de lo que permiten otras tipologías de joya. Como vehículo de conceptos creativos, el broche permite al artista aportar un nivel de profundidad que puede llegar a ser bastante espectacular

En comparación con el anillo, el collar o los pendientes, el broche tiene la cualidad única de ser objeto y joya a la vez. En este sentido el broche representa una hermosa dualidad que no siempre observo en otros tipos de joya, o al menos no del mismo modo. El broche parece tener una raison d'être, es decir, funciona tanto si interactúa con el cuerpo como si no, mientras que otras tipologías parecen estar carentes de algo si el elemento humano no está presente. Quizá esto se puede atribuir en parte al hecho de que el broche no interactúa de manera física con el cuerpo, de manera que no lo necesita para adquirir significado.

Algo que siempre me ha intrigado es que los broches poseen una cierta neutralidad. Cuando creo un broche, nunca pienso si la pieza está destinada a un hombre o a una mujer. Me centro siempre en la creación. Los broches tienden a difuminar los límites de género y son atractivos en función del gusto personal de cada uno, más allá de si son apropiados para un sexo u

otro. Una vez más, quizá esto sea consecuencia del hecho de que el broche no entra en contacto directo con su portador, lo cual hace que el cuerpo pierda importancia en los procesos de diseño y creación. También podría estar relacionado con la idea de que el broche existe, tanto si es llevado como si no.

Uno de los mayores desafíos a los que un artista joyero se enfrenta es la integración del concepto creativo en un objeto llevable, sin que la idea inicial se diluya a lo largo del proceso. Muchos tipos de joyería presentan retos de diseño o restricciones relativas a cómo una determinada pieza se llevará o la sensación que va a proporcionar. Por ello, es posible que partes de la idea inicial queden comprometidas en la transición hacia la funcionalidad y la portabilidad; pero esto rara vez afecta al diseño de un broche, dados los pocos requerimientos que exige su funcionalidad. Al necesitar tan solo una aguja que lo sujete a la prenda, el broche es esencialmente el lienzo en blanco del joyero, mientras cumpla esta única condición.

La naturaleza versátil y dinámica del broche es evidente a través de todo el espectro de la joyería. Los broches se realizan en infinidad de materiales, usando una amplísima variedad de técnicas y poseen las mejores características de la escultura, la arquitectura y la pintura, a escala reducida hasta alcanzar una medida personal e íntima. Los broches hablan de temas y valores sociales y políticos, principios filosóficos y experiencias personales, e indagan en formas geométricas y abstractas. El broche continúa evolucionando y siendo reinterpretado por las manos y las máquinas, y juega un rol fundamental en la evolución de la nueva joyería como plataforma de expresión artística. No ha habido un tiempo mejor que el actual para explorar y documentar los nuevos broches.

AIR

YOJAE LEE
Ichneumon fly
Photo: Kwangchoon Park

Frog skin, leather, silver, gold-plated
polymer clay

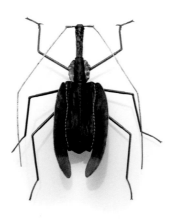

YOJAE LEE
Beetle
Photo: Kwangchoon Park

Frog skin, leather, silver, polymer clay

YOJAE LEE
Mosquito
Photo: Kwangchoon Park

Frog skin, leather, silver, gold-plated
polymer clay

YOJAE LEE
Water stick insect
Photo: Kwangchoon Park

Frog skin, leather, silver, gold-plated
polymer clay

SOL FLORES
Avión 4
Photo: Damian Wasser

Wood, plastic, silver

SOL FLORES
Avión 3
Photo: Damian Wasser

Wood, plastic, nickel silver, pigment

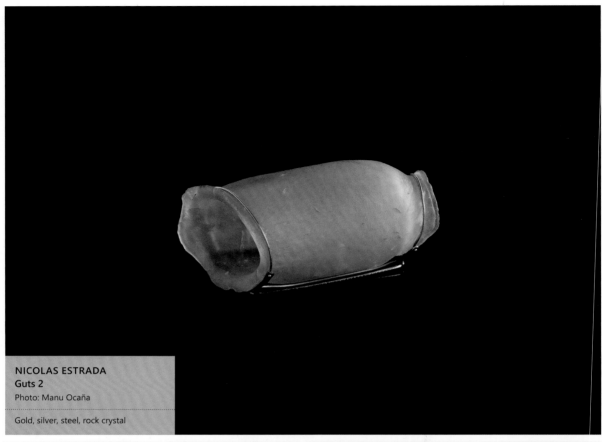

NICOLAS ESTRADA
Guts 2
Photo: Manu Ocaña

Gold, silver, steel, rock crystal

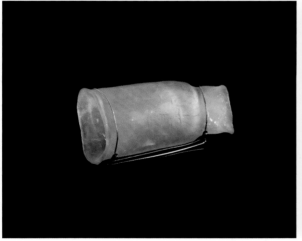

NICOLAS ESTRADA
Guts 1
Photo: Manu Ocaña

Gold, silver, steel, rock crystal

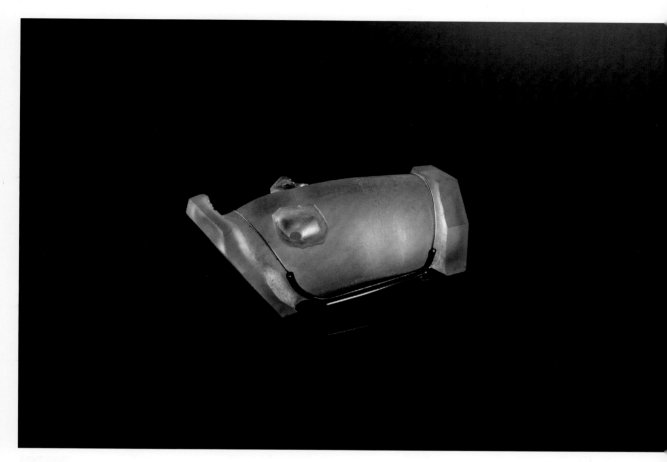

NICOLAS ESTRADA
Spore
Photo: Manu Ocaña

Gold, silver, steel, rock crystal

KARIN ROY ANDERSSON
Steller's Jay
Photo: Karin Roy Andersson

Recycled plastics, steel, tread

KARIN ROY ANDERSSON
Baby Dragon
Photo: Karin Roy Andersson

Recycled plastics, steel, tread

YIOTA VOGLI
Shadow
Photo: Celia Suarez

Wood, acrylics, silver

ANGELA CIOBANU
Piece for the Heart
(Forget-Me-Not series)
Photo: Michael Schindegger

Silver, fine gold Keum-Boo, silk paper,
saw blades

SUSANNE MATSCHÉ
Jewellery Is Social Media
Photo: Johannes Zappe

Silver, steel

SUSANNE MATSCHÉ
Fuck Jewellery
Photo: Johannes Zappe

Silver, steel

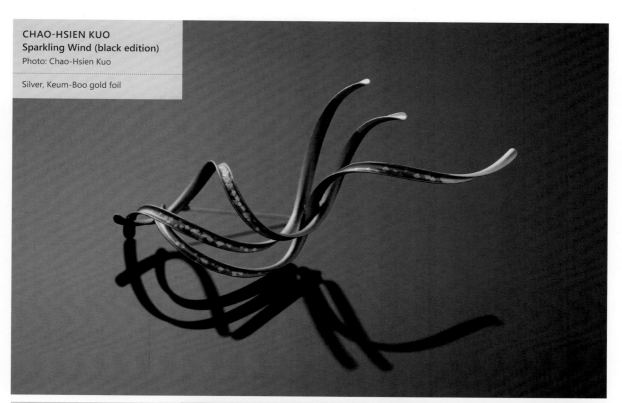

CHAO-HSIEN KUO
Sparkling Wind (black edition)
Photo: Chao-Hsien Kuo

Silver, Keum-Boo gold foil

CHAO-HSIEN KUO
Sparkling Wind
Photo: Chao-Hsien Kuo

Silver, Keum-Boo gold foil

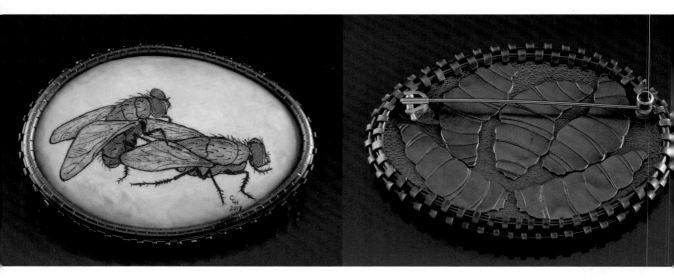

CHARITY HALL
Mating Blowflies
Photo: Charity Hall

Enamel, copper, silver, garnet

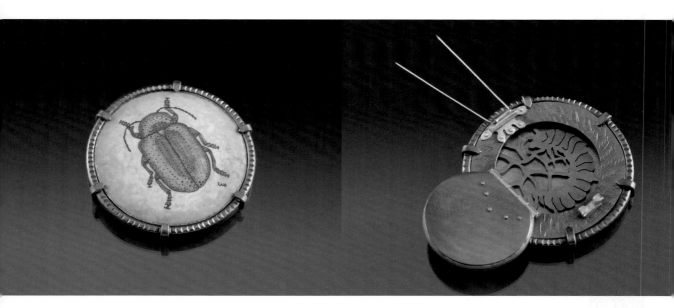

CHARITY HALL
Chrysomelid
Photo: Charity Hall

Enamel, copper, silver, garnet

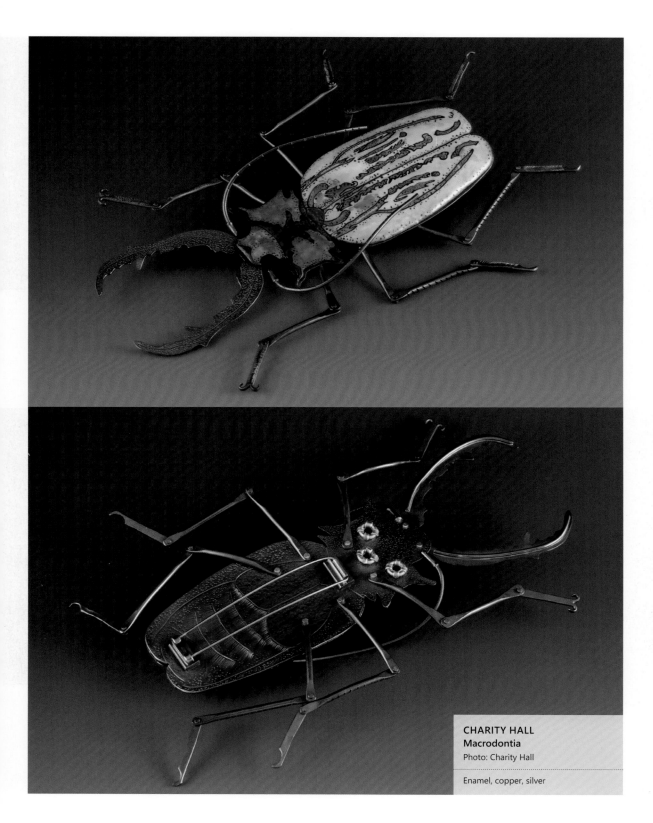

CHARITY HALL
Macrodontia
Photo: Charity Hall

Enamel, copper, silver

LOU SAUTREAU
Extension Brooch
Photo: Valentin Fougeray

Elastomer band, silver, pins

LOU SAUTREAU
Extension Brooch
Photo: Valentin Fougeray

Elastomer band, silver, pins

TYLER STOLL
Green Beanis
Photo: Liz Borsetti

Brass, cement, powder coat, steel,
pigment

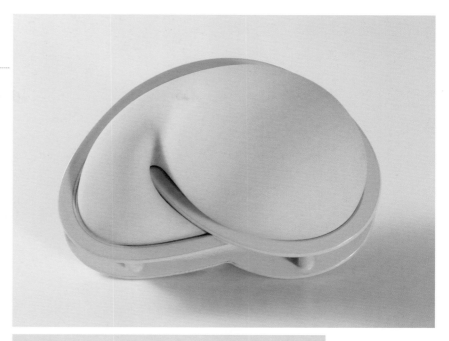

TYLER STOLL
Pink Beanis
Photo: Liz Borsetti

Brass, cement, powder coat, steel,
pigment

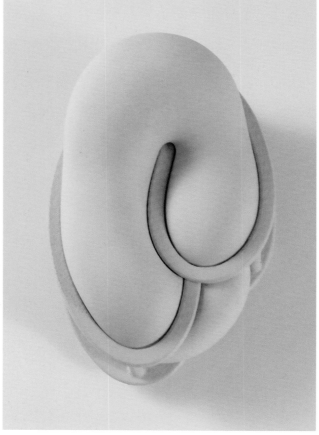

RITA SOTO VENTURA
Refugios I
Photo: Valeska Cirano

Horsehair, vegetal fibre, silver, steel

RITA SOTO VENTURA
Pliegues
Photo: Rita Soto Ventura

Horsehair, vegetal fibre, copper, steel

TITHI KUTCHAMUCH
Travels With My Spoon
Photo: Narut Vatanopas

Silver

KYE-YEON SON
Branch Brooches
Photo: Myung Wook Huh

Copper, enamel

KYE-YEON SON
Innate gesture
Photo: Kye-Yeon Son

Steel, enamel

KYE-YEON SON
Innate gesture
Photo: Myung Wook Huh

Steel

JOANA SANTOS
Urchin – Red Pin
Photo: Nelson Cambão

Silver, nylon, steel

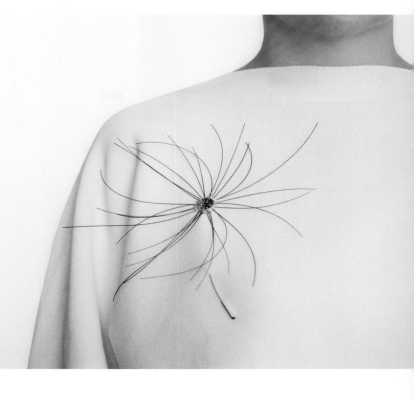

LITAL MENDEL JEWELRY DESIGN
Ephemeral Brooch 1
Photo: Noa Kedmi

Cotton threads, silver, adhesive

DONGYI WU
Dream
Photo: Kanghong Zhong

....

Silver, yarn

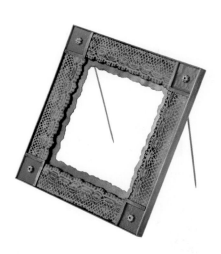

HEIDEMARIE HERB
Collection Minipictures
Photo: Silvana Tili

Silver, brass, pigment

HEIDEMARIE HERB
Brooches
Photo: Silvana Tili

Silver, pigment

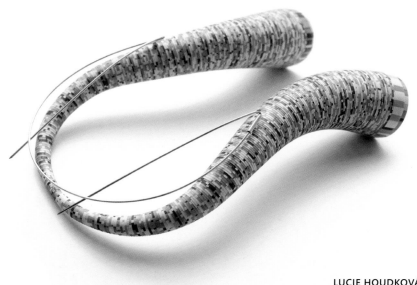

LUCIE HOUDKOVÁ
Formation
Photo: Lucie Houdková

Paper, epoxy, silver, steel

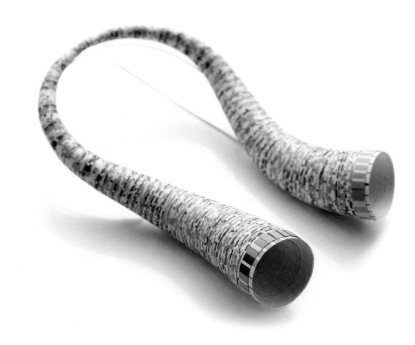

LUCIE HOUDKOVÁ
Deep
Photo: Patrik Borecký, Tomáš Brabec

Paper, silver, steel

DOT.
Sunny Side Up and Running
Photo: Gilad Bar-Shalev

Smoothcast, paint, steel, silver

JULIA HARRISON
1874
Photo: Julia Harrison

Wood, glue, magnet, epoxy

JULIA HARRISON
Cycle
Photo: Julia Harrison

Wood, nickel, glue, oil, wax

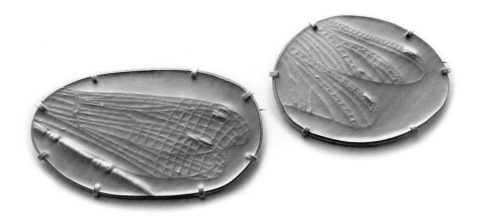

GABRIELE HINZE
Conservatio – Dragonfly
Photo: Ariane Hartmann

Silver, steel

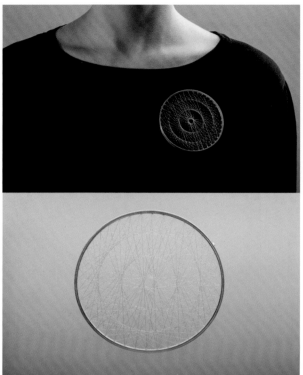

JEANNE MARELL
Spirograph Triple
Photo: Juliet Sheath

Silver, nylon

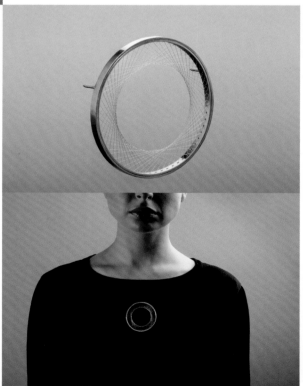

JEANNE MARELL
Spirograph Single
Photo: Juliet Sheath

Silver, nylon

YVONNE GILHOOLY
Hoshi

Photo: Eddy Gallagher

Silver, diamonds, steel

YVONNE GILHOOLY
Maru

Photo: Eddy Gallagher

Gold, steel

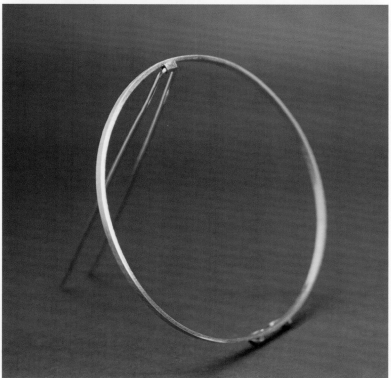

GEORG DOBLER
Brooch
Photo: Georg Dobler

Silver, amethyst

GEORG DOBLER
Brooch
Photo: Georg Dobler

Silver, citrine

GEORG DOBLER
Brooch
Photo: Georg Dobler

Silver, rock crystal

HEEJIN LEE
Peking Euphorbia 1
Photo: KC Studio

Silver

HEEJIN LEE
Peking Euphorbia 2
Photo: KC Studio

Silver

TOMOYO HIRAIWA
Graceful 1
Photo: Shinichi Ichikawa

Silver, pigment

TOMOYO HIRAIWA
Graceful 2
Photo: Shinichi Ichikawa

Silver, pigment

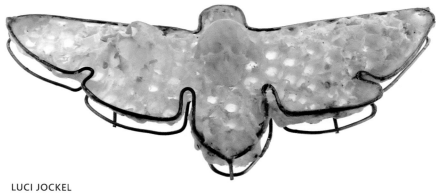

LUCI JOCKEL
Death's Head Hawkmoth
Photo: Luci Jockel

Honeycomb, beeswax, skull, steel, brass

IRIS MERKLE
Le Sacre No.2
Photo: Christoph Binder

Silver, iron, plaster

IRIS MERKLE
Le Sacre No.1
Photo: Christoph Binder

Silver, iron, plaster

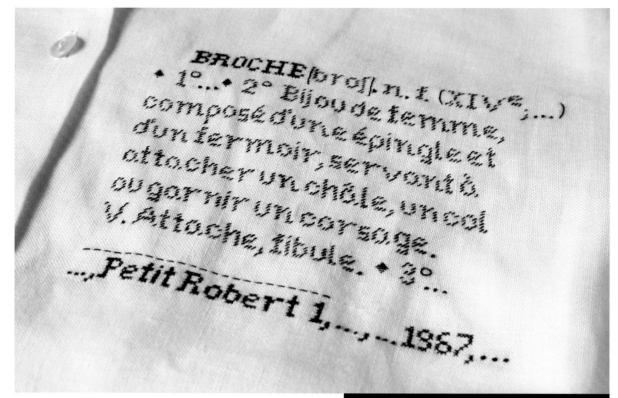

BROCHE (broſ) n. f. (XIVe, …)
◆ 1°… ◆ 2° Bijou de femme,
composé d'une épingle et
d'un fermoir, servant à
attacher un châle, un col
ou garnir un corsage.
V. Attache, fibule. ◆ 3°…
…Petit Robert 1, …, … 1967, …

MONIKA BRUGGER
Inséparable (detail)
Photo: Corinne Janier

Linen, cotton

MONIKA BRUGGER
Inséparable
Photo: Monika Brugger, Corinne Janier

Linen, cotton

UNA MIKUDA
Natural Blond
Photo: Monta Apsane

Silver, linen

CAROLINA BERNACHEA
Fusta
Photo: Carolina Bernachea

Silk thread, silver, steel

JULIA DEVILLE
Bird Shoulder Piece
Photo: Terence Bogue

Taxidermy starling, gold leaf, black sapphires

JULIA DEVILLE
Sparrow Brooch
Photo: Terence Bogue

Taxidermy sparrow, gold, gold leaf, silver, enamel paint

JULIA DEVILLE
Kingfisher
Photo: Terence Bogue

Taxidermy kingfisher wing, silver, enamel paint

CAROLINA BERNACHEA
Lavanda
Photo: Carolina Bernachea

Silk thread, silver, steel, pigments

CAROLINA BERNACHEA
Alma Red
Photo: Carolina Bernachea

Silk thread, silver, steel, pigments

ANNETTE DAM
Transcendence
Photo: Dorte Krogh

Silver, copper, resin

EVA FERNANDEZ MARTOS
Teddy Bear
Photo: Maria Przybylska

Plastic, rubber, brass, paint, steel

PAULA ESTRADA MATYÁŠOVÁ
Anudar - Desanudar
Photo: Juan Fernando Cano

Silver, gold-plated silver

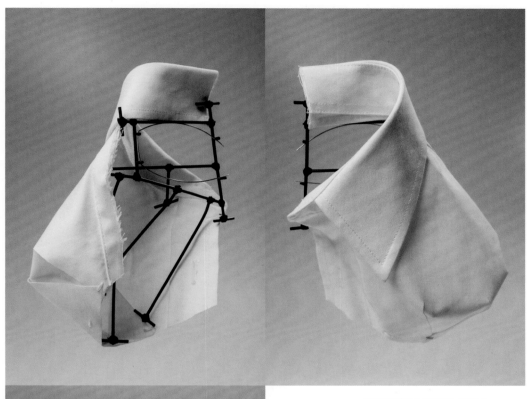

RODRIGO ACOSTA ARIAS
Rito Cardíaco

Photo: Adolfo López

Fabric, brass, cotton thread, steel thread

THEO FENNELL
Crowned Kingfisher

Photo: Hanover Saffron

Gold, sapphires, diamond, ruby,
labradorite

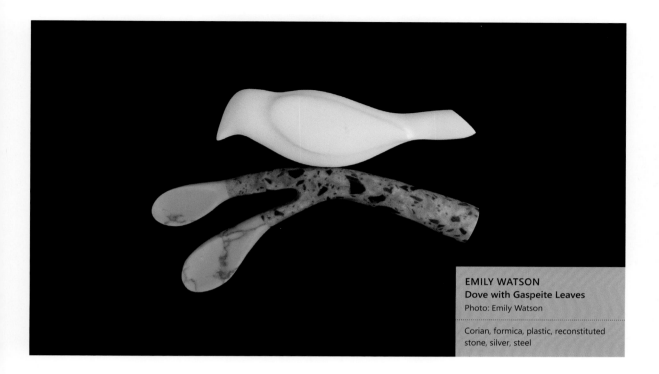

EMILY WATSON
Dove with Gaspeite Leaves
Photo: Emily Watson

Corian, formica, plastic, reconstituted stone, silver, steel

EMILY WATSON
Blue Jay on Branch
Photo: Emily Watson

Corian, formica, reconstituted stone, silver, steel

EMILY WATSON
Yellow Dove
Photo: Emily Watson

Corian, acrylic, silver, steel

HENG LEE
Embroidery – Pixel 3.7 Golden Label
Photo: Heng Lee

Gold-plated steel, thread, organza silk

HENG LEE
Download Nature – Pachliopta Aristolochiae Interpositus
Photo: Heng Lee

Steel, mobile painting, glass bead, thread, silk organza

HENG LEE
Floral Print of Formosa – Lilium Kanahirai
Photo: Heng Lee

Platinum-plated silver, aluminum, paint, thread, organza silk

HENG LEE
Floral Print of Formosa – Pleione formosana
Photo: Heng Lee

Platinum-plated silver, aluminum, paint, thread, organza silk

HENG LEE
Floral Print of Formosa – Delonix Regia
Photo: Heng Lee

Gold-plated silver, aluminum, paint, thread, organza silk

HENG LEE
Embroidery – Pixel 4.1 Golden label
Photo: Heng Lee

Gold-plated steel, thread, organza silk

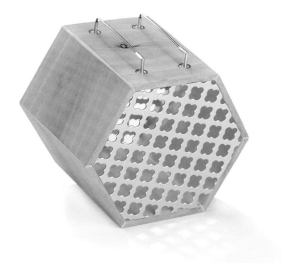

IGNASI CAVALLER
Cannot see further than his nose
Photo: Manu Ocaña

Silver, aluminium, wood, laquer, steel

IGNASI CAVALLER
To cut a flying hair
Photo: Manu Ocaña

Silver, steel, obsidian, flock

KATE DANNENBERG
Pavo Chordata
Photo: Elizabeth Lamark

Copper, brass, peacock feathers, silver

FIRE

THEO SMEETS
TAG & Vulture
Photo: Manu Ocaña

THEO SMEETS
TAG
Photo: Manu Ocaña

Bone, silver, pearls, plastic

THEO SMEETS
Vulture
Photo: Manu Ocaña

Silver, synthetic spinell, garnet, plastic,
steel

TORE SVENSSON
Mr T

Photo: Karin Seufert

Wood, silver, paint

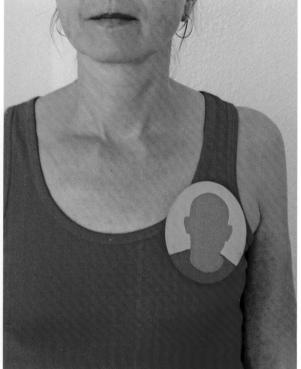

TORE SVENSSON
Mr T

Photo: Tore Svensson

Wood, silver, paint

TSANG-HSUAN LIN
Shifting I
Photo: Tsang-Hsuan Lin

Monel, electronic components, plastic,
steel, paint, prismacolor

TSANG-HSUAN LIN
Shifting II
Photo: Tsang-Hsuan Lin

Monel, electronic components, plastic,
steel, paint, prismacolor

SNEM YILDIRIM
Kanavice
Photo: Snem Yildirim

Brass, plastic, steel

SNEM YILDIRIM
All in One
Photo: Snem Yildirim

Brass, plastic, wood, paint, steel

SNEM YILDIRIM
Three in One
Photo: Snem Yildirim

Brass, plastic, steel

SNEM YILDIRIM
Twiggy
Photo: Snem Yildirim

Brass, plastic, steel

SNEM YILDIRIM
Three of You II
Photo: Snem Yildirim

Brass, plastic, steel

THEO FENNELL
Henry V Skull

Photo: Hanover Saffron

Gold, diamond, mammoth ivory

KIM ERIC LILOT
Medusa's Children
Photo: Hap Sakwa

Black diamonds, rubies, platinum, gold

KIM ERIC LILOT
Medusa's Sword
Photo: Hap Sakwa

Platinum, gold, enamels, sapphire

THEO FENNELL
Henry V Skull (with box)
Photo: Hanover Saffron

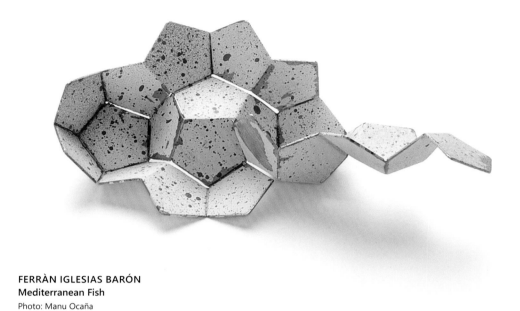

FERRÀN IGLESIAS BARÓN
Mediterranean Fish
Photo: Manu Ocaña

Silver, steel, acrylic paint

FERRÀN IGLESIAS BARÓN
Impression
Photo: Manu Ocaña

Silver, steel, pigment

FERRÀN IGLESIAS BARÓN
Sunflower
Photo: Manu Ocaña

Silver, steel, acrylic paint

HEDVIG WESTERMARK
Empty Black Boxes
Photo: Hans Bjurling

Rubber

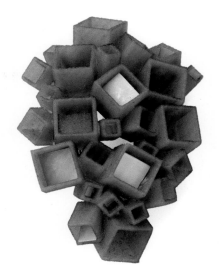

HEDVIG WESTERMARK
Boxes with what remains
Photo: Hans Bjurling

Rubber, gold

HEDVIG WESTERMARK
Boxes in Transition
Photo: Hans Bjurling

Aluminium

JEFFREY LLOYD DEVER
Eden's Harvest – P'installation
Photo: Gregory R. Staley

Wool felt, polymer clay, steel

JEFFREY LLOYD DEVER
Sea Blossom
Photo: Gregory R. Staley

Polymer clay, steel

JEFFREY LLOYD DEVER
As Summer Pales
Photo: Gregory R. Staley

Polymer clay, steel, glass

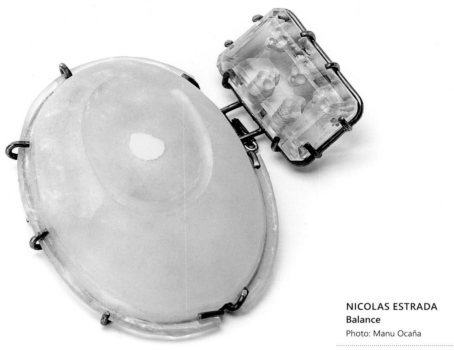

NICOLAS ESTRADA
Balance
Photo: Manu Ocaña

Silver, rose quartz, citrine, steel

KARIM OUKID OUKSEL
Fibula Honey Comb
Photo: Joan Soto

Silver, enamel, coral

MARIA ROSA FRANZIN
La casa dell' anima 8
Photo: Silvano Longo

Silver, acrylic paint

MARIA ROSA FRANZIN
La casa dell' anima 16
Photo: Silvano Longo

Silver, acrylic paint

MARIA ROSA FRANZIN
La casa dell' anima 14
Photo: Silvano Longo

Silver, acrylic paint

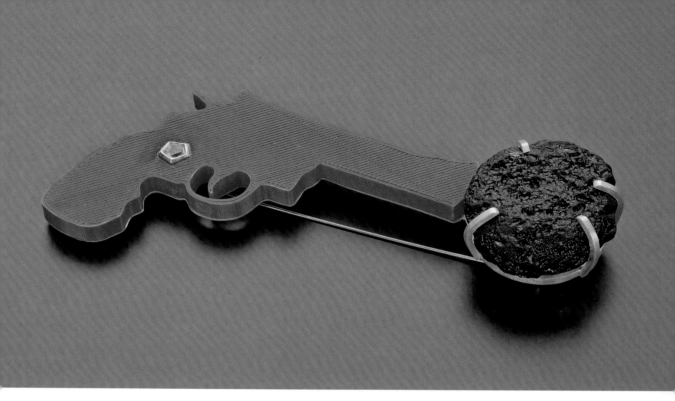

BABETTE VON DOHNANYI
Our World

Photo: Federico Cavicchioli

Silver, corn, rock crystal, tektite, steel

PAULA ZUKER
Broche 3
Photo: Damian Wasser

Porcelain, enamel, silver

TOVE KNUTS
DBET KMG30
Photo: Tove Knuts

Leather, wool filling, brooch needle

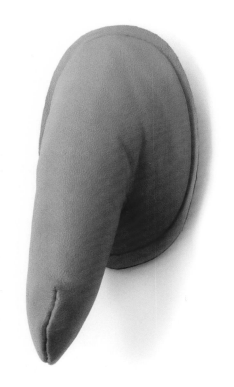

**DAUVIT ALEXANDER – THE
JUSTIFIED SINNER**
Verklärte Nacht
Photo: Simon Murphy

Found corroded iron barbed wire, silver,
diamonds, labradorite

**DAUVIT ALEXANDER – THE
JUSTIFIED SINNER**
Verklärte Nacht
Photo: Andrew Neilson, Neilson
Photography

Found corroded iron barbed wire, silver,
diamonds, labradorite

**DAUVIT ALEXANDER – THE
JUSTIFIED SINNER
Blood Will Have Blood – A
MacBeth Brooch**

Photo: Andrew Neilson, Neilson
Photography

Found corroded tank cap, silver, obsidian,
polycarbonate, quartz, garnets

**DAUVIT ALEXANDER – THE
JUSTIFIED SINNER
Blood Will Have Blood – A
MacBeth Brooch**

Photo: Simon Murphy

Found corroded tank cap, silver, obsidian,
polycarbonate, quartz, garnets

PATRICIA LÓPEZ PIEDRAHITA
Bordar el corazón 1
Photo: Coque Gamboa

Wood, silver, thread

PATRICIA LÓPEZ PIEDRAHITA
Volver a casa 2
Photo: Coque Gamboa

Wood, silver, thread

JULIA KRAEMER-LOSEREIT
Red Orange Round 0317
Photo: Julia Krämer-Losereit

Silver, thread

JULIA KRAEMER-LOSEREIT
Colorful Oval 0317
Photo: Julia Krämer-Losereit

Silver, thread

JULIA KRAEMER-LOSEREIT
Yellow Grey Oval 0317
Photo: Julia Krämer-Losereit

Silver, thread

ANNA DAVERN
Nagging
Photo: Terence Bogue

Reworked biscuit tin, printed steel,
copper, garnet and ruby beads

ANNA DAVERN
The Duke of Devonshire
Photo: Anna Davern

Reworked biscuit tin, printed steel,
copper, garnet and ruby beads

ANNA DAVERN
Knight Commander
Photo: Anna Davern

Reworked biscuit tin, printed steel,
copper, garnet and ruby beads

ANNA DAVERN
**The Treasurer of His Majesty's
Household**
Photo: Anna Davern

Reworked biscuit tin, printed steel,
copper, garnet and ruby beads

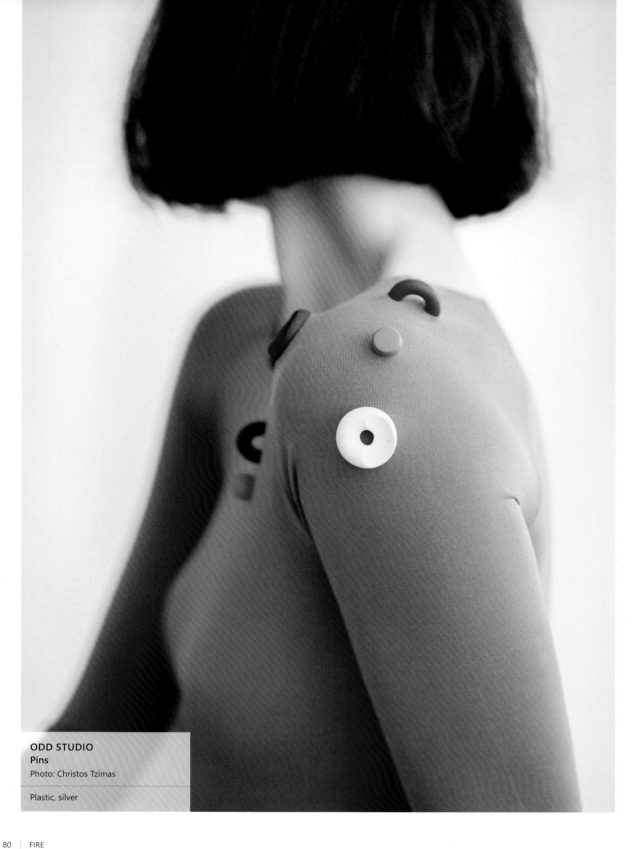

ODD STUDIO
Pins
Photo: Christos Tzimas

Plastic, silver

ODD STUDIO
Ovule 1
Photo: Christos Tzimas

Plastic, silver

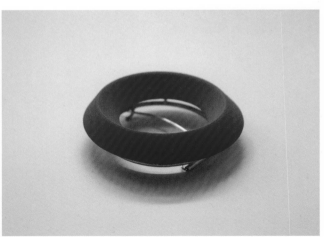

ODD STUDIO
Will 2
Photo: Vasilis Aggelopoulos

Plastic, magnet

ODD STUDIO
Breath 2
Photo: Vasilis Aggelopoulos

Plastic, magnet

RALPH BAKKER
Bonding 3
Photo: Michael Anhalt

Tantalum, gold

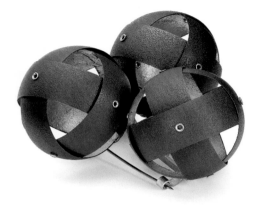

RALPH BAKKER
Bonding 1
Photo: Michael Anhalt

Tantalum, gold

RALPH BAKKER
Bonding 2
Photo: Michael Anhalt

Gold, silver

EZRA SATOK-WOLMAN
Nautilus Carboniferous
Photo: Ezra Satok-Wolman

Carbon fibre, gold, palladium, Tahitian
pearl, Paraiba tourmaline

EZRA SATOK-WOLMAN
Lumina
Photo: Ezra Satok-Wolman

Gold, thread

MLLE GUILLAUME
La Boite en Carton

Photo: Poptown Photo

Enamel on copper, silver, gold,
powdercoat, steel

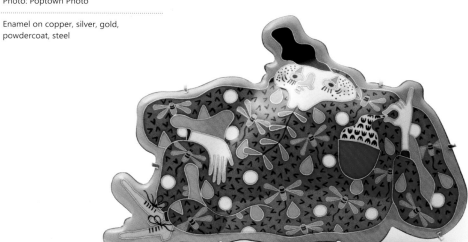

MLLE GUILLAUME
La Bibitte

Photo: Anthony Mc Lean

Enamel on copper, silver, gold,
powdercoat, steel

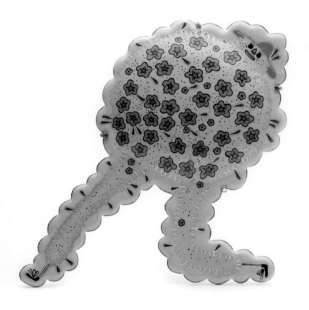

MLLE GUILLAUME
Puff Puff

Photo: Anthony Mc Lean

Enamel on copper, silver, powdercoat, steel

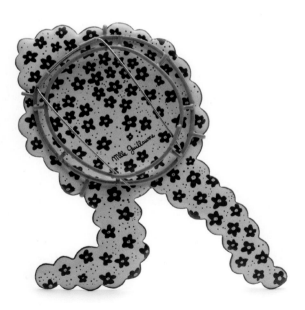

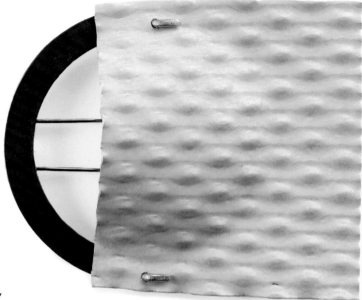

STEPHEN BOTTOMLEY
Lemon Yellow
Photo: Shannon Tofts

Silver, enamel, gold, steel

STEPHEN BOTTOMLEY
Heat Exchanger
Photo: Shannon Tofts

Copper, brass, peacock feathers, silver

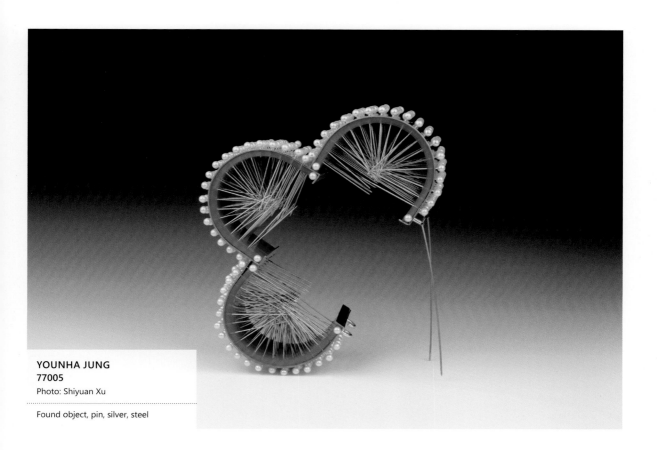

YOUNHA JUNG
77005
Photo: Shiyuan Xu

Found object, pin, silver, steel

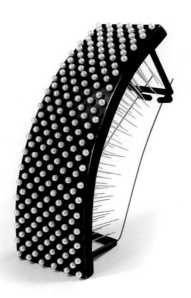

YOUNHA JUNG
Untitled 41
Photo: Younha Jung

Brass, rubber, steel, pearl

EMILY PELLINI
Swarming Brooch Series – Swarming
Photo: Emily Pellini

Copper, powder coat, silver, steel,
vitreous enamel

EMILY PELLINI
Swarming Brooch Series – Regret
Photo: Emily Pellini

Copper, powder coat, silver, steel,
vitreous enamel

EMILY PELLINI
Swarming Brooch Series – Discovery
Photo: Emily Pellini

Copper, powder coat, silver, steel,
vitreous enamel

YI-JEN CHU
Untitled 2
Photo: Yi-Jen Chu

Copper, brass, plastic, steel

YI-JEN CHU
Untitled 3
Photo: Yi-Jen Chu

Copper, brass, plastic, steel

JOY-JO (GIOVANNA CANU)
Mouth-Shaped Brooche
Photo: Eleonora Marangon

Copper, garnet

LETICIA LLERA MARTÍNEZ
Movimientos
Photo: Meli Poggi

Silver

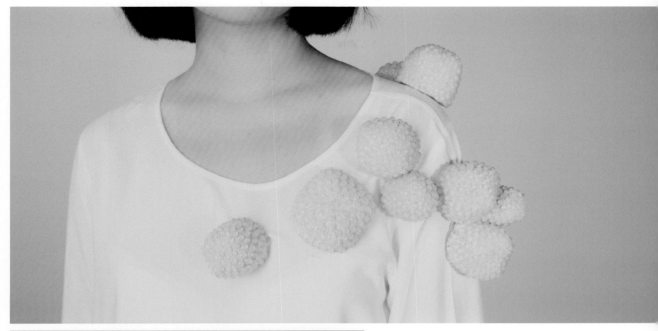

HELMI LINDBLOM
Fruitfully Yours – Fertility
Photo: Ninni Vidgren

Balloons, resin, polymer, silicon, silver

HELMI LINDBLOM
Fruitfully Yours – Fertility
Photo: Ninni Vidgren

Balloons, resin, polymer, silicon, silver

FELIEKE VAN DER LEEST
Brachiosaurus tree with UFO nest
and alien eggs
Photo: Eddo Hartmann

Argentium®, textile, plastic animal, glass
beads, leather, magnets

FELIEKE VAN DER LEEST
Brachiosaurus tree with UFO nest
and alien eggs
Photo: Eddo Hartmann

Argentium®, textile, plastic animal, glass
beads, leather, magnets

FELIEKE VAN DER LEEST
Spermheart Rocker
Photo: Eddo Hartmann

Silver, textile, plastic animal, cubic
zirconia

FELIEKE VAN DER LEEST
Lunatitia Velociraptorina
Photo: Eddo Hartmann

Argentium®, textile, plastic animal, cubic
zirconia

FELIEKE VAN DER LEEST
Mr. Zen
Photo: Eddo Hartmann

Textile, plastic animal, mother of pearl,
glass, silver

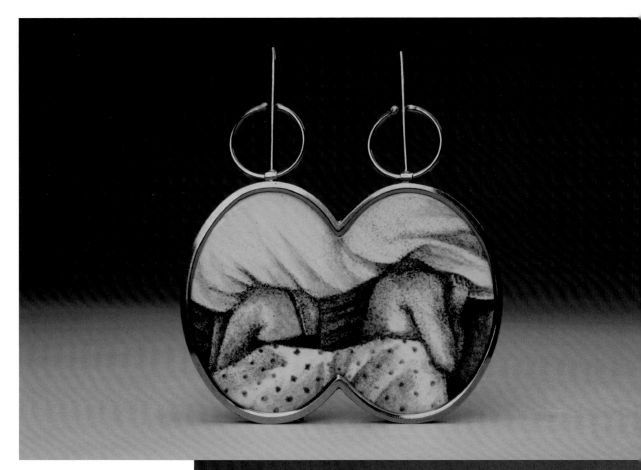

JESSICA CALDERWOOD
Domestication
Photo: Jessica Calderwood

Enamel, copper, silver, china paint

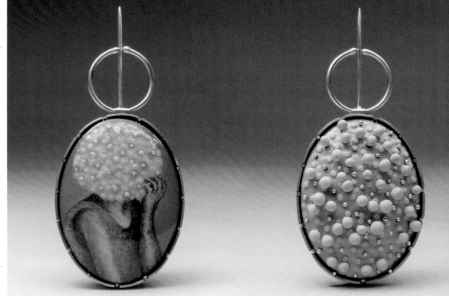

JESSICA CALDERWOOD
Fret
Photo: Jessica Calderwood

Enamel, copper, silver, polymer clay,
glass beads, china paint

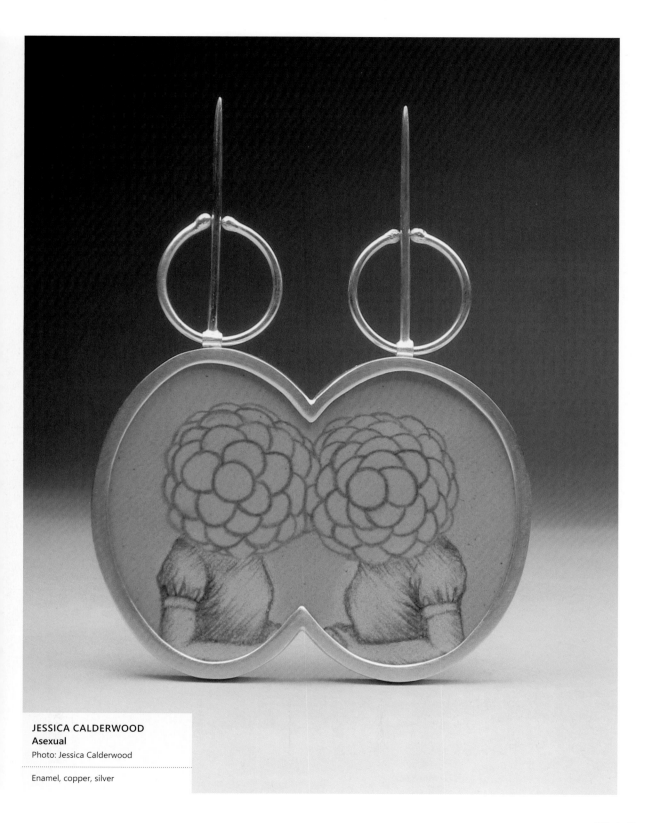

JESSICA CALDERWOOD
Asexual
Photo: Jessica Calderwood

Enamel, copper, silver

JAKI COFFEY
SOS 1

Photo: Damien Maddock

....

Nylon, steel, wadding and reflective tape

MELISSA CAMERON
11 RPH Cannon

Photo: Melissa Cameron

Vintage Japanese lacquer ware plate, thread, copper

THEO SMEETS
Baltic Bite
Photo: Manu Ocaña

Amber, plastic, porcelain, steel

ELIN FLOGNMAN
Barber's Knife
Photo: Elin Flognman

Wood, steel, paint

ELIN FLOGNMAN
Kitchen Knife
Photo: Elin Flognman

Wood, steel, paint

ELIN FLOGNMAN
Carving Knife
Photo: Elin Flognman

Wood, steel, paint

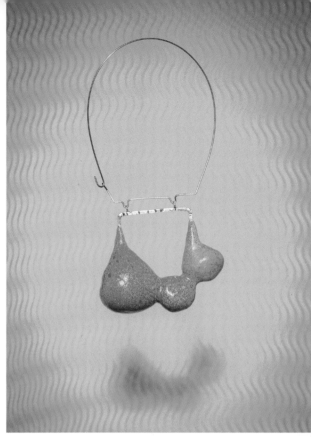

HANNAH-MAY CHAPMAN
My Pair
Photo: www.greenlandphotography.com

Silver, steel, tin, polymer clay, paint,
lacquer

HANNAH-MAY CHAPMAN
My Wave
Photo: www.greenlandphotography.com

Silver, steel, tin, polymer clay, paint,
lacquer

LENA WUNDERLICH
Eye, eye
Photo: Anna Shapiro

Copper, brass, paint, steel

LENA WUNDERLICH
Invisible Whiteness
Photo: Anna Shapiro

Copper, brass, paint, steel

DOT.
Hallo Kitty 2
Photo: Dot Visual

Bone, silver, plastic, wood, glass, rock
crystal, fungus, hair, leafs, wings

LUCI JOCKEL
Bloom
Photo: Josephine Hjort

Groundhog skull, honey comb, beeswax,
tree fungi, brass, steel

GREGORY LARIN
With all my
Photo: Dima Reinshtein

Polymer, steel, brass, pigment, leather

EARTH

ALŽBĚTA DVOŘÁKOVÁ
The Secret of Space
Photo: Lenka Grabicová

Gold leaf, leather, silver, brass

MARION BLUME
Branch – no branch 06
Photo: Bastian Schultes

Wood, silver, remanium

MARION BLUME
Branch – no branch 08
Photo: Bastian Schultes

Wood, silver, remanium

MARION BLUME
Branch – no branch 07
Photo: Bastian Schultes

Wood, silver, remanium

JULIA HARRISON
Corsage
Photo: Julia Harrison

Wood, steel, urethane, epoxy

JULIA HARRISON
Consolation
Photo: Julia Harrison

Wood, nickel, oil, wax, epoxy

JULIA HARRISON
Swallowtail
Photo: Julia Harrison

Wood, nickel, paint, epoxy, wax

JULIA HARRISON
Low Rise
Photo: Julia Harrison

Wood, nickel, paint, epoxy, wax

JULIA HARRISON
Formline
Photo: Julia Harrison

Wood, nickel, paint, epoxy, wax

NICOLE TAUBINGER
**Will you take me out for dinner,
Mr. Warhol?**
Photo: Kamil Till

Plastic rubbish

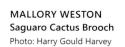

MALLORY WESTON
Saguaro Cactus Brooch
Photo: Harry Gould Harvey

Copper, paint, nickel, polyester, cotton
thread

YIQING CAI
Lung Branching
Photo: Anastasia Tres

Brass

YIQING CAI
Lung Branching
Photo: Anastasia Tres

Brass

TAMARA GRÜNER
Karpador
Photo: Alexander König

Iron and manganese oxid, bone, silver, glass, plastic, steel

TAMARA GRÜNER
Savanna
Photo: Alexander König

Galalithe, kyanite, silver, glass, plastic, steel

WENDY MCALLISTER
Thistle
Photo: Victor Wolansky Photography

Vitreous enamel, copper, silver, gold

WENDY MCALLISTER
Polar Vortex
Photo: Victor Wolansky Photography

Vitreous enamel, copper, silver, glass

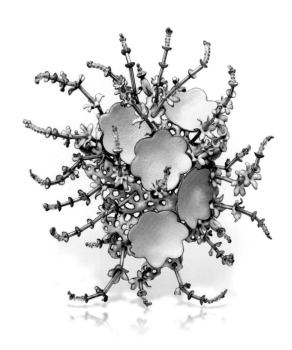

JORGE CASTAÑÓN
¿Cuánto pesa la ausencia?
What's the weight of absence?
Photo: Damián Wasser

Wood, silver

JORGE CASTAÑÓN
Titicaca I
Photo: Damián Wasser

Wood, silver

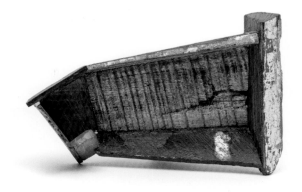

JORGE CASTAÑÓN
Vacío
Photo: Damián Wasser

Wood, silver

JORGE CASTAÑÓN
Aguamarina
Photo: Damián Wasser

Wood, silver

NATALIE HOOGEVEEN
Oh Deer!

Photo: Saskia Wagenvoort

Silver, pearls, woood, plastic, gemstones, shells, glass

GERTI MACHACEK
Hekate
Photo: Toni Pölzl

Bone, silver, steel

KARIN SEUFERT
n.T.372
Photo: Karin Seufert

PVC, polystyrene, silver, steel

KARIN SEUFERT
n.T.346
Photo: Karin Seufert

PVC, paper, steel

EDNA MADERA
Extract Study 03
Photo: Cole Rodger

Gold, silver

HADAS LEVIN
Road Marks I-V
Photo: Hadas Levin

Steel, enamel

SHARON MASSEY
Brickwork: Puff
Photo: Sharon Massey

Copper, enamel, silver, steel

SHARON MASSEY
Brickwork: Twist
Photo: Sharon Massey

Copper, enamel, silver, steel

PAMELA DE LA FUENTE
Imagen Devocional 2
Photo: Lucas Nuñez

Oil painted wood, credit cards

PAMELA DE LA FUENTE
Imagen Devocional 1
Photo: Lucas Nuñez

Enameled copper, Social Security card

XENIA WALSCHIKOW
Painted flower in quinacridone pink & cadmium red orange
Photo: Jonny Wilson

Paint, silver

JAN SMITH
Marked 1&2
Photo: Gillean Proctor

Silver, copper, vitreous enamel, steel

JAN SMITH
Marked Mended Stitched Group 20
Photo: Gillean Proctor

Silver, copper, vitreous enamel, steel

KATIE STORMONTH
Dual Longline Fan Brooches
Photo: Faun Photography

Silver, aluminium, steel, wood, paint

TARA LOCKLEAR
Rubble of Gems Fuchsia Pile
Photo: Tara Locklear

Recycled broken skateboards, wood,
pigment, silver, steel

TARA LOCKLEAR
**Rubble of Gems Turquoise
Baby Pile**
Photo: Tara Locklear

Recycled broken skateboards, wood,
pigment, silver, steel

TARA LOCKLEAR
Rubble of Gems Olive Pile
Photo: Tara Locklear

Recycled broken skateboards, wood, pigment, silver, steel

CRISTINA ZANI
My Seoul – wood and patina
Photo: Cristina Zani

Brass, gold leaf, coconut wood

BABETTE VON DOHNANYI
Darkness
Photo: Federico Cavicchioli

Gold, jet

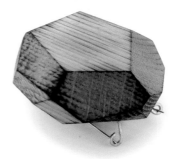

BABETTE VON DOHNANYI
Rocks
Photo: Federico Cavicchioli

Gold, wood

EVA BURTON
Das Autito
Photo: Eva Burton

Reclaimed wood, cachalong, recon, paper, acrylic paint, steel

EVA BURTON
Das Autito
Photo: Eva Burton

Reclaimed wood, cachalong, recon, paper, acrylic paint, steel

PATRÍCIA DOMINGUES
Duality Series
Photo: Patrícia Domingues

Necuron, steel

PIERO ACUTO
Baboja 2
Photo: Piero Acuto

Aluminium, steel

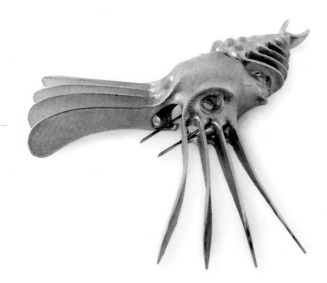

PIERO ACUTO
Baboja 4
Photo: Piero Acuto

Aluminium, steel, brass

PIERO ACUTO
Baboja 3
Photo: Piero Acuto

Aluminium, steel

FLORENCIA INÉS ALONSO
Calma
Photo: Damian Wasser

Iron, wood, cotton thread, silver

FLORENCIA INÉS ALONSO
Esperanza
Photo: Damian Wasser

Wood, cotton thread, silver

COVA RÍOS
ArBoReM
Photo: Luis Rubín

Silver, steel, rock crystal

JUHANI HEIKKILÄ
Midsummer
Photo: Rauno Träskelin

Wood

JUHANI HEIKKILÄ
Pig
Photo: Rauno Träskelin

Wood

ANJA EICHLER
Tree of Life
Photo: Anja Eichler

Quail eggs, silver, twig, steel wire,
silver wire

ANJA EICHLER
Silence 4
Photo: Anja Eichler

Cuttlefish bone, silver, steel wire

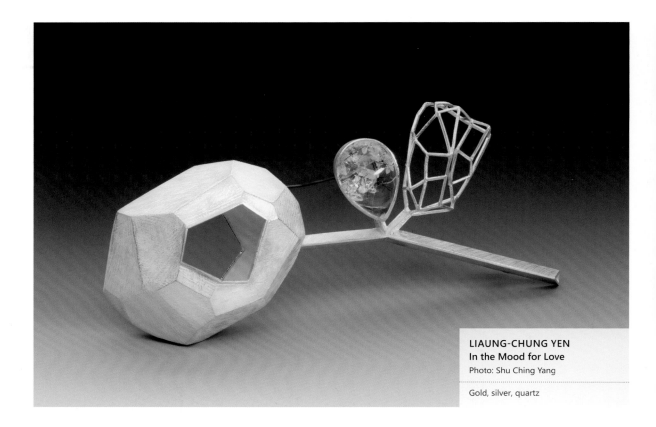

LIAUNG-CHUNG YEN
In the Mood for Love
Photo: Shu Ching Yang

Gold, silver, quartz

ROBYN WILSON
Brooches x 4
Photo: Screaming Pixels

(L-R) Silver, citrine / Silver, amethyst /
Silver, gold Keum-Boo, peridot / Monel,
silver, meteorite

MARTA ROCA SOLÉ
Topografías
Photo: Mª del Mar Campano

Paper, silver, steel

EUNSEON PARK
Bouquet
Photo: Grace Laemmler

Copper, powder coat, gold leaf, steel

EUNSEON PARK
Bouquet
Photo: Grace Laemmler

Copper, powder coat, gold leaf, steel

WALKA
(CLAUDIA BETANCOURT + NANO PULGAR)
Andes Series
Photo: Karen Clunes

Horn, silver, gold

KAREN VANMOL
Cultivate 2
Photo: Karen Vanmol

Wood, laminate, steel, silver, brass, paint

KAREN VANMOL
Cultivate 5
Photo: Karen Vanmol

Wood, laminate, steel, silver, brass, paint

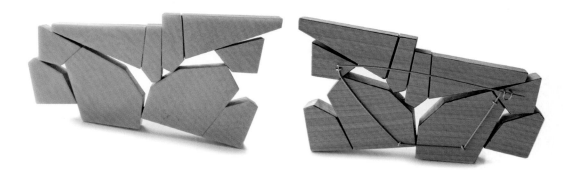

KAREN VANMOL
AKA # Iseefaces 1
Photo: Karen Vanmol

Wood, laminate, steel

SHARAREH AGHAEI
Untitled
Photo: Nima Ashrafi

Iron, silver, acrylic, cement, resin, steel

SHARAREH AGHAEI
Untitled
Photo: Sharareh Aghaei

Silver, copper, enamel, acrylic, resin, steel

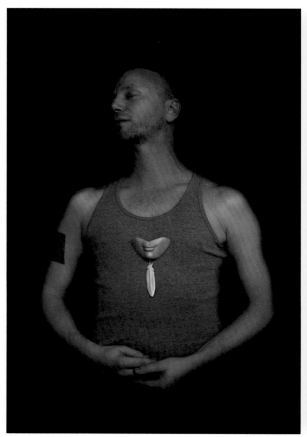

TANEL VEENRE
Mutual Hearts X
Photo: Tanel Veenre

Wood, camel bone, silver, cosmic dust

TANEL VEENRE
Mutual Hearts IV
Photo: Tanel Veenre

Shells, camel bone, resin, silver, cosmic dust

TANEL VEENRE
**Rabbit who doesn`t know weather
to be gray or pink**
Photo: Tanel Veenre

Wood, resin, silver, cosmic dust

TANEL VEENRE
Red Rabbit
Photo: Tanel Veenre

Wood, reconstructed coral, resin, silver,
cosmic dust

BARBARA PAGANIN
Memoria Aperta
Photo: Alice Pavesi Fiori

Silver, gold, porcelain, ivory, tourmaline,
coral, miniature, photograph, glass

BARBARA PAGANIN
Memoria Aperta No. 19
Photo: Alice Pavesi Fiori

Silver, ivory, gold, tourmaline

BARBARA PAGANIN
Memoria Aperta No. 4
Photo: Alice Pavesi Fiori

Silver, glass, gold, porcelain, tourmaline,
photograph

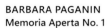

BARBARA PAGANIN
Memoria Aperta No. 1
Photo: Alice Pavesi Fiori

Silver, gold, porcelain, tourmaline,
rubies

CRISTINA ZANI
My Seoul – grey and gold
Photo: Cristina Zani

Gold plated silver, wood, paint,
gold leaf

CRISTINA ZANI
My Seoul – red and patina
Photo: Cristina Zani

Patinated brass, wood, paint

SIM LUTTIN
Relic No. 9
Photo: Andrew Barcham

Wood, silver, steel

SIM LUTTIN
Relic No. 1
Photo: Andrew Barcham

Wood, silver, steel

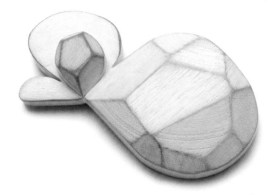

SIM LUTTIN
Relic No. 13
Photo: Andrew Barcham

Wood, silver, steel

GABRIELE HINZE
Blossombranch
Photo: Georg Eichinger

Silver, steel, synthetics

GABRIELE HINZE
Blossombranch
Photo: Georg Eichinger

Silver, steel, synthetics

PAUL MCCLURE
Flora: Splice
Photo: Norman Wong

Silver, nylon

PAUL MCCLURE
Flora: Spray
Photo: Digital by Design

Silver, nylon

ROSA NOGUÉS FREIXAS
Nautilus
Photo: Carles Fargas

Copper, enamel, silver, steel

ROSA NOGUÉS FREIXAS
Fosco
Photo: Carles Fargas

Silver, steel

NICO SALES
Oh, paradís!
Photo: Helena Pons Sans

Silver, rubber, steel, polycarbonate, daffodil

 ETHER

GÉSINE HACKENBERG
Unballanced Rotation
Photo: Gésine Hackenberg

Porcelain, pigment, silver, steel

GÉSINE HACKENBERG
Sweeping Out
Photo: Gésine Hackenberg

Porcelain, pigment, silver, steel

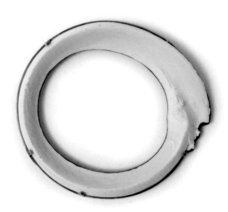

GÉSINE HACKENBERG
Swinging Out
Photo: Gésine Hackenberg

Earthenware, glaze, silver, steel

YIOTA VOGLI
Secrets
Photo: Celia Suarez

Paper pulp, acrylics, silver, nickel silver, brass

JAMES DUNN
Tank

Photo: James Dunn

Steel

JAMES DUNN
Mitered

Photo: James Dunn

Steel

CAMILLA LUIHN
It's Complicated
Photo: Camilla Luihn

Copper, champlevé vitreous enamel, steel

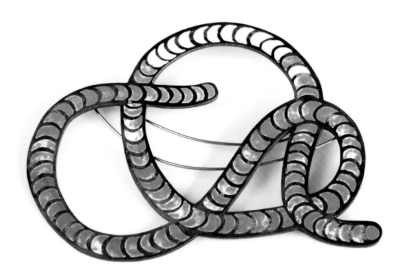

CAMILLA LUIHN
Red Spring
Photo: Jan Alsaker

Copper, silver

ANGELA BUBASH
Fin No. 30
Photo: Mary Vogel

Silver, glass, feathers

ANGELA BUBASH
Fin No. 48
Photo: Angela Bubash

Silver, glass, green chalcedony,
dyed feathers

SIM LUTTIN
Melancholy: These Things That Never Were
Photo: Andrew Barcham

Silver, hematite, onyx, steel

SIM LUTTIN
Moment No. 1
Photo: Andrew Barcham

Gold, silver, steel, rock crystal Silver, glass, paper, gold, steel

LLUÍS COMÍN
Barcino 1
Photo: Carles Fargas

Silver, jasper, gold, steel, patinas

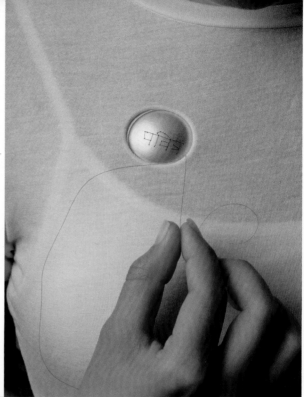

PALLAVI VERMA
Holy
Photo: Nanó Wallenius

Hair, gold, rhodium-plated silver

PALLAVI VERMA
Joystick (switches)
Photo: Laurent-Max De Cock

Rhodium-plated silver, magnets

PAUL FRANCIS ADIE
Fruit from the Wasteland III
Photo: Paul Andrew Adie

Steel

PAUL FRANCIS ADIE
The Earth is Moving III
Photo: Mirei Takeuchi

Steel

GIGI MARIANI
Reperto 281016
Photo: Paolo Terzi

Silver, gold, niello, patina

GIGI MARIANI
Painting series No. 2
Photo: Paolo Terzi

Silver, gold, niello, patina

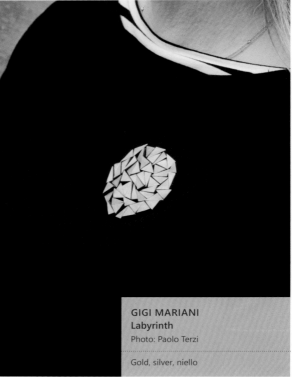

GIGI MARIANI
Labyrinth
Photo: Paolo Terzi

Gold, silver, niello

**SUPERLORA STUDIO
BY ARIADNE KAPELIOTI
Future 02**

Photo: Superlora Studio

Steel, rubber, aluminium, nylon, bronze

EVGENIIA BALASHOVA
Cable Management Brooch
Photo: Valentina Pimanova

Nylon, spray paint, sterling silver,
stainless steel pin

JO POND
The Prince Albert Assemblage
Photo: Jo Pond

Repurposed tins, steel,
Victorian silver coin.

HIND ELHAFEZ
Sea Froth
Photo: Zeina Abaza

Food can, silver, wax paint, steel

HIND ELHAFEZ
Bubblegum
Photo: Zeina Abaza

Food can, silver, wax paint, steel

HIND ELHAFEZ
Dark Forest
Photo: Zeina Abaza

Food can, silver, wax paint, steel

HIND ELHAFEZ
Old Gold
Photo: Zeina Abaza

Food can, silver, wax paint, steel

MAREEN ALBURG DUNCKER
Petrol
Photo: Nils Kinder

Enameled and gold-plated copper, gold,
steel

MAREEN ALBURG DUNCKER
Yellow
Photo: Nils Kinder

Enameled and silver-plated copper,
silver, steel

FELIEKE VAN DER LEEST
Ki-mini: brooch
with exchangeable dresses
Photo: Eddo Hartmann

Silver, textile, glass beads

ERICA BELLO
Brooches for the Superstitious
Photo: Erica Bello

Oxidized silver, steel pin wire

CURTIS H. ARIMA
Disorder
Photo: Curtis H. Arima

Silver, gold, amethyst, garnets,
diamonds

CURTIS H. ARIMA
Edwardian Purple
Photo: Eric Smith

Silver, gold, amethysts, diamonds

UTE DECKER
Dancing Spiral
Photo: Ute Decker

Silver

UTE DECKER
Crest of Waves at Noon
Photo: Ute Decker

Gold

EMILY COBB
Tangled Up: The Hare
Photo: Emily Cobb

Nylon, acrylic, silver

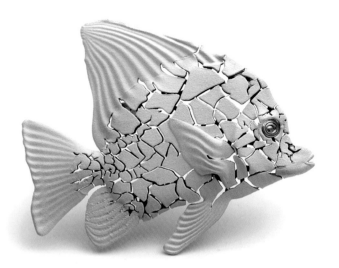

EMILY COBB
Dry Up: Tropical Fish
Photo: Emily Cobb

Nylon, acrylic, silver

EMILY COBB
Tangled Up: Black Mouse
Photo: Emily Cobb

Nylon, acrylic, pearl

EMILY COBB
Dry Up: Anchovy
Photo: Emily Cobb

Nylon, acrylic, silver

 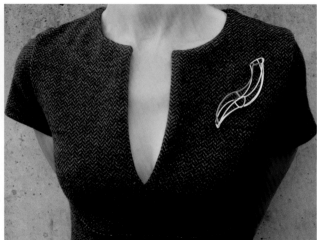

VERONIEK DUTRÉ
Monkey Puzzle
Photo: Veroniek Dutré

Copper, silver, paint

VERONIEK DUTRÉ
Monkey Puzzle
Photo: Veroniek Dutré

Copper, silver, paint

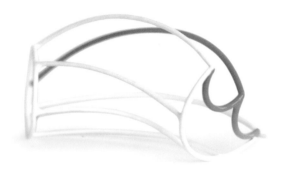

MONIKA BRUGGER
Gothic Attribut(s)
Photo: Corinne Janier, Paris

Silver, Rhodium-plated silver, gold,
stainless steel, fabric, gold, steel, fabric

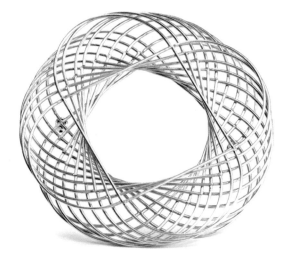

EZRA SATOK-WOLMAN
Ultralight Beams No. 3
Photo: Ezra Satok-Wolman

Platinum

EZRA SATOK-WOLMAN
Ultralight Beams No. 2
Photo: Ezra Satok-Wolman

Platinum

TALA YUAN
Rest Space
Photo: Tala Yuan

Arkansas stone, tiger eye, metal net,
silver

TALA YUAN
Travel in the World Sea
Photo: Tala Yuan

Pink quartz, agate, porcelain, steel

T SQUARED BY TAMI ESHED
Recycled Powder
Photo: Dima Reinshtein

Silver, brass, paint powder

T SQUARED BY TAMI ESHED
Recycled Powder
Photo: Dima Reinshtein

Silver, brass, paint powder

JÁNOS GÁBOR VARGA
Lobe
Photo: Luca Orlandini

Copper, steel

JÁNOS GÁBOR VARGA
Pierce
Photo: Luca Orlandini

Iron, silver, gold

JÁNOS GÁBOR VARGA
Odyssey
Photo: Luca Orlandini

Iron, gold

SAMUEL GUILLÉN
Untitled
Photo: Arturo Sanchez

Silver, black diamonds, steel

SAMUEL GUILLÉN
Untitled
Photo: Arturo Sanchez

Silver, gold

SAMUEL GUILLÉN
Untitled
Photo: Arturo Sanchez

Silver, steel

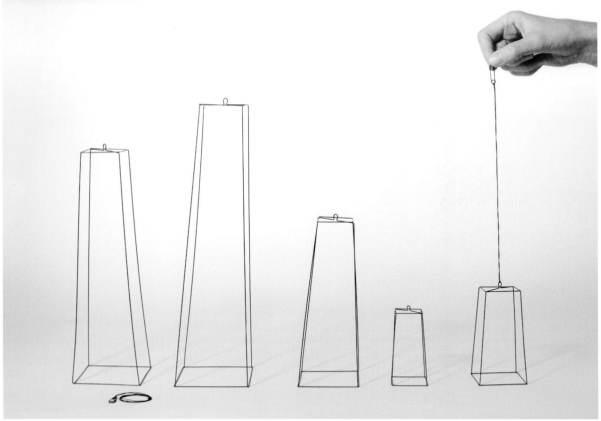

CÉLINE SYLVESTRE
Silhouette – series
Photo: Matthieu Gauchet

Iron, silk thread

ESTELA SAEZ VILANOVA
Solitud
Photo: Jordi Puig

Silver

KATJA PRINS
Hybrid 03
Photo: Merlijn Snitker

Chrome-plated brass, resin

KATJA PRINS
Hybrid 14
Photo: Merlijn Snitker

Chrome-plated brass, resin

SONDRA SHERMAN
Rorschach Corsage: Belladonna II
Photo: Luna Perri

Steel, gold

SONDRA SHERMAN
Rorschach Corsage: Valerian II
Photo: Luna Perri

Steel

FERNANDA MITSUE
Soul
Photo: Lívia Fernandes

Gold-plated brass

MARIA DIEZ SERRAT
Tijeras de punta
Pointed Scissors
Photo: Maria Diez Serrat

Brass

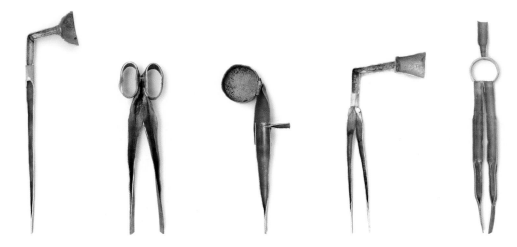

MARIA DIEZ SERRAT
Sense mesura series
Without Measure series
Photo: Maria Diez Serrat

Brass

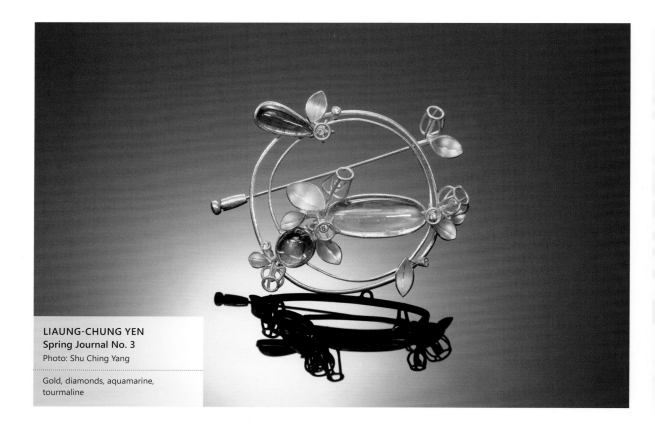

LIAUNG-CHUNG YEN
Spring Journal No. 3
Photo: Shu Ching Yang

Gold, diamonds, aquamarine,
tourmaline

ANGELA BUBASH
Ephemeral Resonance – Dove
Photo: Mary Vogel

Silver, glass, dyed cotton, scent

LUCIE MAJERUS
Human Ivory
Photo: Matan Bellemaker

Silver, personal teeth

WATER

ANTRIA PRASINOU
Liberate the Senses
Photo: Konstantinos Kostopoulos

Rice paper, ink, finger prints, thread,
cane, silver

JULIA MARIA KÜNNAP
Why is it all overgrowing
Photo: Julia Maria Künnap

Nephrite, gold

JULIA MARIA KÜNNAP
Nubis
Photo: Ulvi Tiit

Obsidian, gold

JULIA MARIA KÜNNAP
Molten
Photo: Ulvi Tiit

Smoky quartz, gold

RAMÓN PUIG CUYÀS
Subtle Architectures series
Photo: Ramón Puig Cuyàs

Nickel silver

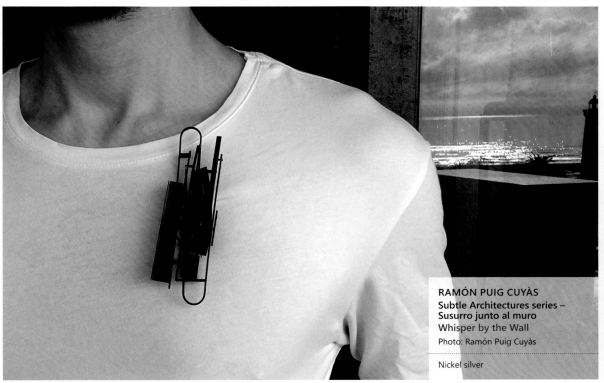

RAMÓN PUIG CUYÀS
Subtle Architectures series –
Susurro junto al muro
Whisper by the Wall
Photo: Ramón Puig Cuyàs

Nickel silver

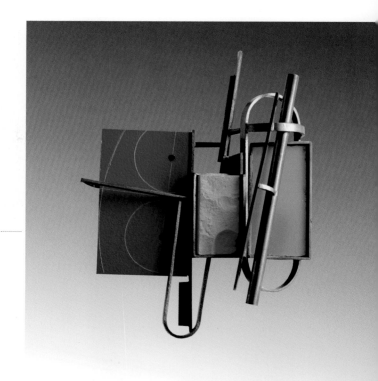

RAMÓN PUIG CUYÀS
Subtle Architectures series
Photo: Ramón Puig Cuyàs

Nickel silver, enameled steel,
ColorCore, reconstituted turquoise

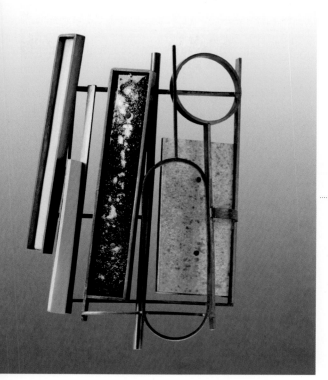

RAMÓN PUIG CUYÀS
Subtle Architectures series
Photo: Ramón Puig Cuyàs

Nickel silver, enameled steel, plastic

JOSHUA KOSKER
Be Gentle
Photo: Joshua Kosker

Soap, silver, steel

JOSHUA KOSKER
[re]embody
Photo: Joshua Kosker

Soap, copper, steel, silver

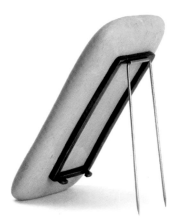

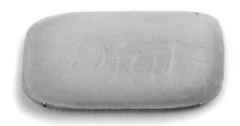

JOSHUA KOSKER
Dial
Photo: Joshua Kosker

Soap, silver, steel

JOSHUA KOSKER
Nestle
Photo: Joshua Kosker

Soap, silver, steel

MAGALI THIBAULT GOBEIL
Joy and Rainbow Cloud
Photo: Alexis Kamitsos

Polyurethane, vinyl, thread, cotton, magnet

MAGALI THIBAULT GOBEIL
Afro-candy or «Moi je suis dans le vent!»
Photo: Anthony McLean

Polyurethane, vinyl, thread, cotton, magnet

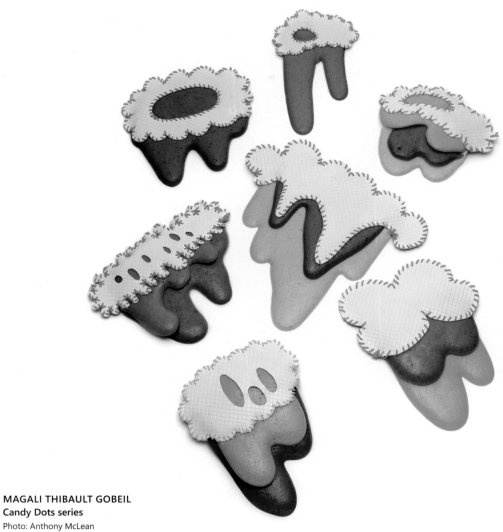

MAGALI THIBAULT GOBEIL
Candy Dots series
Photo: Anthony McLean
....

Polyurethane, vinyl, thread, cotton,
magnet

CHRISTINE JALIO
Past, Loss, Future
Photo: Anne Ruotsalainen

Silk clay, foam clay, silver, steel

CHRISTINE JALIO
Past, Loss, Future
Photo: Maarit Halonen

Silk clay, foam clay, silver, steel

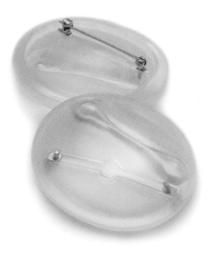

ANGELA BUBASH
Two Brooches Inside a Jewellery Box
Photo: Lin Cheung

Quartz, gold

ROBERT THOMAS MULLEN
Mineral
Photo: Robert Thomas Mullen

Calcite, plastic, nickel, silver, paint

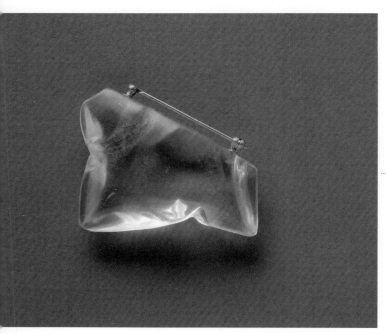

LIN CHEUNG
Corner of a Plastic Bag
Photo: Lin Cheung

Quartz, gold

ARTEMIS VALSAMAKI
Sleep Like an Angel
Photo: Alexis Kamitsos

Copper, silver, acrylic

ARTEMIS VALSAMAKI
We Come in Peace
Photo: Alexis Kamitsos

Copper, silver, acrylic, flock, plexiglas

ARTEMIS VALSAMAKI
Self-fish

Photo: Alexis Kamitsos

Copper, silver, acrylic, mirror

ARTEMIS VALSAMAKI
Hypnagogia

Photo: Alexis Kamitsos

Copper, silver, acrylic

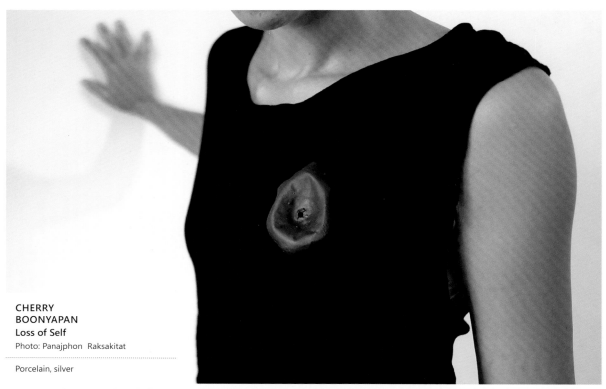

**CHERRY
BOONYAPAN**
Loss of Self
Photo: Panajphon Raksakitat

Porcelain, silver

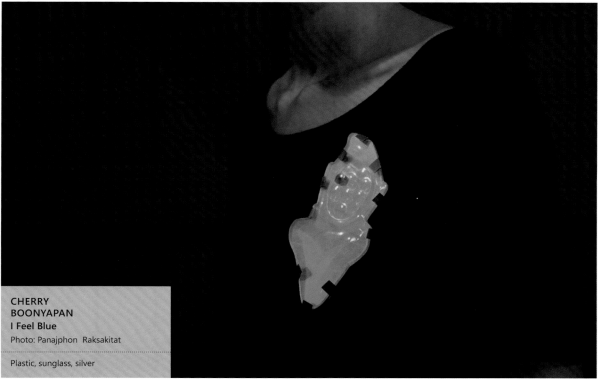

**CHERRY
BOONYAPAN**
I Feel Blue
Photo: Panajphon Raksakitat

Plastic, sunglass, silver

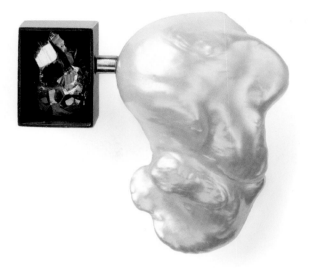

HEDVIG WESTERMARK
A Perfect Couple
Photo: Hans Bjurling

Silver, gold, pyrite, fresh water pearl

HEDVIG WESTERMARK
A Small Collection
Photo: Hans Bjurling

Silver, gold, coral, South Sea pearl

GÉSINE HACKENBERG
Tumbling Pink Glass
Photo: Gésine Hackenberg

Theresienthal glassware, silver

GÉSINE HACKENBERG
Tumbling Yellow Glass
Photo: Gésine Hackenberg

Theresienthal glassware, silver

GÉSINE HACKENBERG
Still Life Composition
Photo: Thomas Heere

Vintage table glasses, silver

GÉSINE HACKENBERG
Tableau Vivant with Kitchen Glass Brooches
Photo: Karin Nussbaumer

Kitchen glassware, silver

JOSE LUIS FETTOLINI
Space Invader
Photo: Panajphon Raksakiat

Methacrylate

WILLIAM RUDOLPH FAULKNER
A Sharp Rise
Photo: William Rudolph Faulkner

Glass, silver, steel

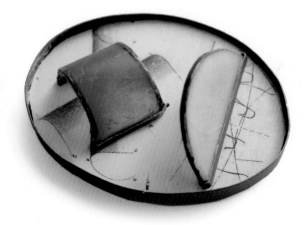

SILVIA WALZ
Geometría de la luz
Photo: Silvia Walz

Steel, enamel

SILVIA WALZ
Absorption
Photo: Silvia Walz

Steel, enamel

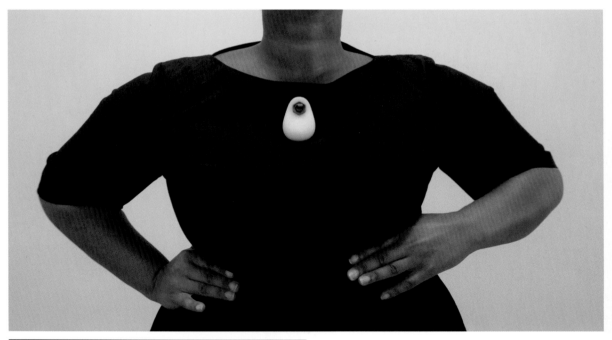

HELEN HABTAY
Turn Me On, Switch Me Off, No. 3
Photo: Helen Habtay

Pink marble, switch, steel

JULIA OBERMAIER
It's Always Changing
Photo: Julia Obermaier

Agate, resin, pigment, steel

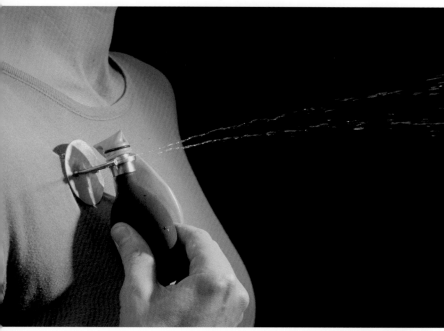

SIGURD BRONGER
Carrying device for a balloon
Photo: Sigurd Bronger

Gold-plated brass, steel, rubber

SIGURD BRONGER
Carrying device for a natural yellow sponge
Photo: Sigurd Bronger

Gold-plated brass, steel , rubber tube and pump

MONTSERRAT LACOMBA
Life's Moments series
Photo: Josep M. Oliveras

Enameled copper, silver

CAMILLA LUIHN
I Question Your Perception of Air, 1 – 6
Photo: Camilla Luihn

Silver, glass, dyed cotton, scent

ISABELLE BUSNEL
L205
Photo: Yiannis Katsaris

Silicone rubber, magnets

ISABELLE BUSNEL
K33
Photo: Yiannis Katsaris

Silicone rubber, magnets

ISABELLE BUSNEL
K39
Photo: Yiannis Katsaris

Silicone rubber, magnets

JULIA BAUDLER
Blue'n'Tourquoise
Photo: Sarah Beekmann

Silver, resin

JULIA BAUDLER
Growing
Photo: Sarah Beekmann

Silver, eggshell, resin, rock crystal

ANYA KOVALIEVA - OLL
Crease
Photo: Anya Kovalieva

Polymer, brass

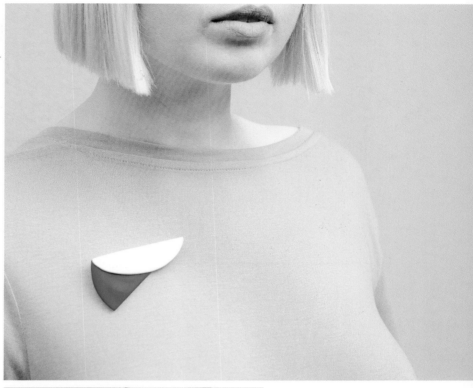

ANYA KOVALIEVA - OLL
Crease
Photo: Anya Kovalieva

Polymer, brass

BIBA SCHUTZ
Thumbalina
Photo: Ron Boszko

Silver, borosilicate glass

BIBA SCHUTZ
Brooch 1
Photo: Ron Boszko

Silver, glass

BIBA SCHUTZ
Beutts
Photo: Ron Boszko

Silver, black glass

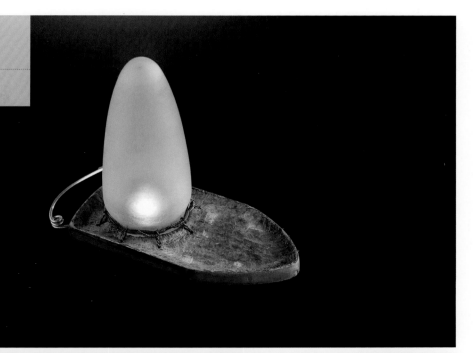

NICOLAS ESTRADA
Kap Arkona
Photo: Manu Ocaña

Silver, rock crystal, wood, electric
components

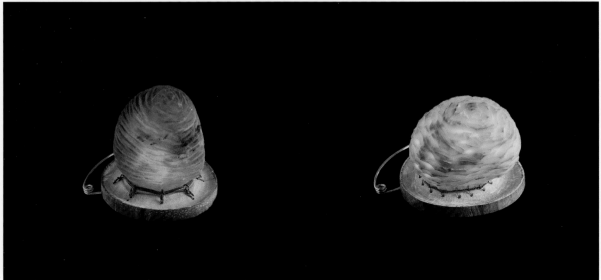

NICOLAS ESTRADA
Dornbusch
Photo: Manu Ocaña

Silver, rock crystal, wood, electric
components

NICOLAS ESTRADA
Gellen
Photo: Manu Ocaña

Silver, vegetable ivory, electric
components

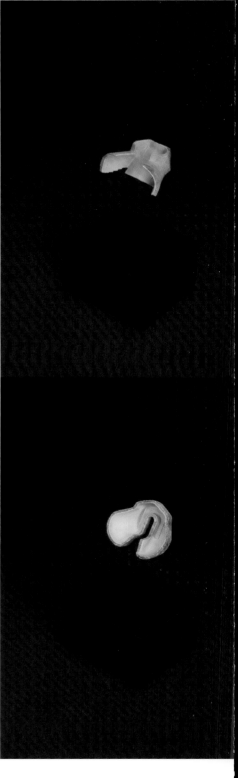

EDU TARIN
Mold A2
Photo: Edu Tarin

Jasper, copper, gold

EDU TARIN
Mold A2
Photo: Edu Tarin

Jasper, copper, gold

EDU TARIN
Mold E2
Photo: Edu Tarin

Jasper, copper, gold

CHRISTOPH STRAUBE
Brooch
Photo: Christoph Straube

Steel, enamel

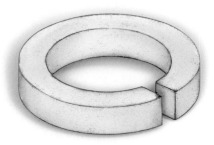

CHRISTOPH STRAUBE
Brooch
Photo: Christoph Straube

Steel, enamel

CHRISTOPH STRAUBE
Brooch
Photo: Christoph Straube

Steel, enamel

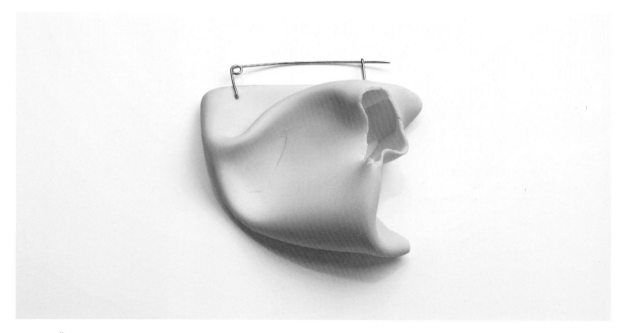

SELEN ÖZUS
The Closest
Photo: Umut Töre

Porcelain, gold

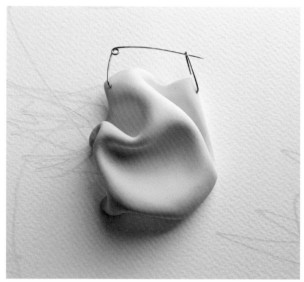

SELEN ÖZUS
The Closest
Photo: Umut Töre

Porcelain, gold

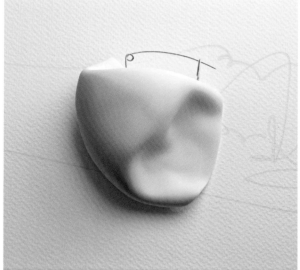

SELEN ÖZUS
The Closest
Photo: Umut Töre

Porcelain, gold

WENDY MCALLISTER
Blue Penta Hydra
Photo: Victor Wolansky Photography

Vitreous enamel, copper, silver

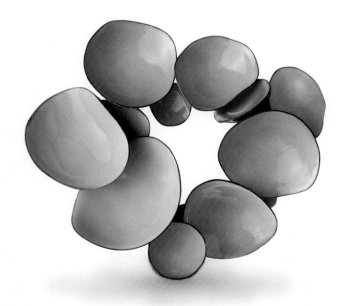

WENDY MCALLISTER
Robin Eggs
Photo: Victor Wolansky Photography

Vitreous enamel, copper, silver

DONALD FRIEDLICH
Celery
Photo: Larry Sanders

Glass, gold

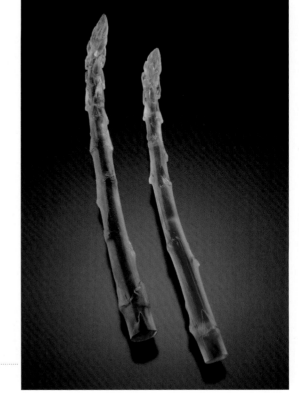

DONALD FRIEDLICH
Asparagus
Photo: Larry Sanders

Glass, gold

UNA MIKUDA
Air – Breath – Wind – Fragility
Photo: Una Mikuda

Copper, enamel, silver

ABOUT THE AUTHOR

Nicolas Estrada

Nicolas Estrada was born in Medellín in 1972, but he discovered his artistic pathway in Barcelona, a city that he had come to for entirely different reasons.

Until that point, he had been an inhabitant of the business world, where he was involved in marketing. His destiny, however, was to follow another path: creating one-off jewellery artworks that were meaningful, unique and infused with stories that speak to the senses.

At Barcelona's Llotja and Massana schools, he came into contact for the first time with the jewellery world, in which he discovered that his efforts opened up infinite possibilities for expression. A tireless researcher of his craft, his curiosity and his passion for this discipline have led him into different territories via a path toward seeking balance and perfection. He has studied widely, learning the techniques of gemology, setting and engraving, and producing research and works through his involvement in areas such as the traditional Berber jewellery of Kabylia, filigree techniques learned in the Colombian town of Santa Cruz de Mompox, and master's-level studies in gemstone cutting and jewellery design at the University of Trier in Germany.

The subjects that Nicolas takes inspiration from for his pieces directly address the humanity and sensibility of those who view them. His pieces do not seek to defend or take positions on situations that are undeniably central and significant in his country and his continent. Instead, they are the pure and clear gaze of an artist who seeks, through the tools offered by his artistic work, to provide new perspectives. For Nicolas, each piece of jewellery is imbued with immense power and value. The poetry contained in Nicolas's work emerges through interpreting his artistic reflections, which are conveyed in an intimate dialogue between the object and the other's gaze. What Nicolas offers us is an extraordinary and provocative ode to irreverence and reflection that is expressed in the aura of a craft undertaken judiciously and based on profound thought.

Nicolas is the author of four books on jewellery that have been published by Promopress in several languages and distributed worldwide: New Rings; New Earrings, New Necklaces, and a revised and updated edition of his first book on rings, which was co-published by Thames & Hudson.

Nicolas lives in Barcelona, the city that allowed him to be who he wanted to be and to do what he wanted to do. He has his own studio, where he shares his craft and experiences with other jewellers who live in or are passing through this wonderful city.

Nicolas Estrada | p. 69

SOBRE EL AUTOR

Nicolas Estrada

Nicolas Estrada (Medellín, 1972) descubre el camino de su arte en Barcelona, a donde otras muy distintas razones lo habían llevado.

Su mundo hasta entonces había sido el de un empresario dedicado al campo del marketing. Su destino, sin embargo, habría de llevarlo por otras sendas: la creación de joyas llenas de significado, piezas de arte únicas, plenas de historias sensibles.

En las escuelas Llotja y Massana de Barcelona tuvo sus primeros contactos con el universo de la joyería, en cuya labor descubrió un mundo de infinitas posibilidades de expresión. Investigador incansable de su oficio, su curiosidad y su pasión por esta disciplina lo han conducido por diferentes geografías a través de su camino de equilibrio y perfeccionamiento; llevándolo a realizar diversos estudios, pasando por las técnicas de gemología, engastado, cincelado, hasta realizar investigaciones y trabajos en campos como la joyería tradicional bereber de la Kabylia, la técnica de filigrana, en la población colombiana de Santa Cruz de Mompox y una maestría de bellas artes en talla de piedras preciosas y diseño de joyería en la Universidad de Trier en Alemania.

Los temas que Nicolas Estrada toma como inspiración para sus piezas tratan directamente la humanidad y la sensibilidad de sus observadores, no son piezas en las que se busque defender o tomar posiciones respecto a situaciones que indu-

dablemente tienen un peso y una trascendencia innegable para su país y su continente, sino que son la mirada pura y clara de un artista que busca así, con las herramientas que su trabajo artístico le ofrece, aportar nuevas perspectivas. Para Nicolas, cada joya está cargada de inmenso poder y valor. Una propuesta poética como la contenida en la obra de Nicolas Estrada converge en la lectura de una reflexión artística plena de significado y fuerza, lo que se traduce en un diálogo íntimo entre el objeto y la mirada del otro. Nicolas nos ofrece algo extraordinario y provocador, un canto a la irreverencia y a la reflexión, rodeado por el aura de una disciplina juiciosamente llevada a cabo y profundamente pensada.

Nicolas Estrada es autor de cuatro libros de joyería publicados por Promopress en varios idiomas y distribuidos por todo el mundo: Anillos – 500 creaciones artísticas de todo el mundo, Pendientes – 500 creaciones artísticas de todo el mundo, Collares – 400 nuevos diseños en joyería contemporánea y la edición revisada y actualizada de su primer libro sobre anillos, publicada por Thames & Hudson.

Nicolas reside en Barcelona, la ciudad que le permitió ser quien quiso ser y hacer lo que quiso hacer. Tiene su propio taller en el que comparte oficio y vivencias con otros joyeros que residen o van de paso por esa maravillosa ciudad.

INDEX OF ARTISTS // ÍNDICE DE ARTISTAS

>> A >>

Alžběta Dvořáková Prague,Czech Republic > p. 106
alz.dvorakova@gmail.com | www.alzbetadvorakova.cz
Alžběta Dvořáková was born in Prague, Czech Republic. She studied at three art schools, two of which focused on jewellery studies and utilitarian arts. Her diploma graduation work was awarded the 2016 Marzee International Graduate Prize by Gallery Marzee. She works with many different materials, and especially with leather, wood and metal. She also likes to use less durable materials such as paper and gold leaf. The key aspects of her work are the ways in which her jewellery pieces connect with and touch the viewer/wearer.

Angela Bubash Rice, Virginia, USA > p. 158, 188, 201
angelabubash@gmail.com | www.angelabubash.com
Angela Bubash is a studio jeweller and educator who resides in Rice, Virginia, where she currently teaches at Longwood University and maintains her own studio practice. She received a BFA from Edinboro University of Pennsylvania and an MFA from Southern Illinois University Carbondale. She completed her residency at Penland School of Crafts in North Carolina, and she has exhibited her work nationally and internationally.
Exploring the intersection of past and present is an ongoing challenge that drives her research and keeps her work on the cusp of dialogue. Encased natural or found objects feature prominently in her work, along with vials, pomanders and reliquaries. By using both visual and olfactory ephemera, each piece examines the precariousness of memory and the human impulse toward nostalgia.

Angela Ciobanu Bucharest, Romania / Residing in Vienna > p. 19
studio@angelaciobanu.ro | press@angelaciobanu.ro | www.angelaciobanu.ro
Angela's interest in contemporary jewellery emerged as a result of the natural change of scale that she initially had the chance to experience in the larger – dimensionally speaking – context of architecture. Her jewellery mirrors her fascination with imperfections, and it features surprising details placed in apparently conventional shapes. She never ceases to search for the unexpected strengths that lie in fragility and lightness. Currently living and working in Vienna, she was born in 1984 in Bucharest, where she would later graduate from the Ion Mincu University of Architecture. She created her first piece of jewellery in March 2010 – a ring that she lost a month later in an airport.

Anja Eichler Düsseldorf, Germany / Residing in Berlin, Germany > p. 133
www.anjaeichler.com
As a child, Anja dreamed of two things: being an artist, and leaving her home country to live abroad and explore the world. Both dreams came true at some point: she has lived in the United States, Italy and China, and she studied jewellery at Alchimia in Firenze. All these experiences have left traces in her work. Anja uses materials from everyday life. We are so familiar with such items that they do not seem to offer any surprises, but what fascinates Anja is that there is a lot to discover in them once we start to look closely and find new potential in things that we think that we know so well.

Anna Davern Melbourne, Australia > p. 78-79
annadavern@me.com | annadavern.com.au
Anna Davern gained her undergraduate degree from Sydney College of the Arts in 1993 and completed her master's degree at RMIT in 2003. She has held three solo exhibitions at Craft Victoria in Melbourne and has been represented in numerous solo and group exhibitions. In 2011, she cofounded Northcity4, an ARI in Melbourne that provides professional and creative opportunities to the contemporary jewellery community. She has been the recipient of grants from the Australia Council, Arts Victoria and NAVA, and in 2007 she undertook a residency at the Estonian Academy of Art. Anna has taught and lectured at universities and TAFEs in Australia and overseas.

Annette Dam Aarhus, Denmark / Residing in Copenhagen, Denmark > p. 47
mail@annettedam.dk | www.annettedam.dk
Annette Dam studied at the Oslo National Academy of the Arts in Norway. She works as a jeweller and coordinates exhibitions around the world. Annette has received multiple grants from the Danish Art Foundation. She has been shown at Schmuck and awarded several prizes over the years. Her work involves a meeting of the artistic, the conceptual and the handmade, and her investigative practices make an active contribution to the design and final expression of her pieces. Her jewellery is created within a sensual and narrative universe in which elements of seriousness are combined with a sense of humour. The themes within her work are considered through a perspective that is both loving and critical, and her aim is to produce communicative artistic jewellery.

Antria Prasinou Athens, Greece > p. 192
antriaprasinou@gmail.com | www.antriaprasinou.com
Antria Prasinou studied graphic design in Athens and attended courses on jewellery casting with D. Nikolaidis and on handmade jewellery design with Lila de Tsaves at the Benaki Museum. She has exhibited at the Sieraad International Jewellery Exhibition in Amsterdam and at Inhorgenta. In Athens, she has taken part in many contemporary jewellery design exhibitions such as Tools at The Arts Foundation and Symbols at Technopolis, and she also participated in the first Athens Jewellery Week at Melanithros Art Space. Her work can be found in selected stores in Athens, Cyprus, Belgium, Germany and Italy, as well as at the Benaki Museum in Athens.

Anya Kovalieva Belarus / Residing in Newcastle upon Tyne, UK > p. 215
hello@ollthethings.com | www.ollthethings.com
Carefully made and exquisitely finished by hand, every piece of Anya Kovalieva's jewellery speaks of her excitement about and devotion to form and colour. During her training as an artist and photographer at Valand Art Academy in Sweden, Anya longed to make things that would be used. For two years, she designed and made contemporary solid wood furniture. However, attracted by the possibilities of using more colours and abstract shapes, she switched her medium to jewellery, which she produces under the brand name Oll. Her pieces are both strong and serene, and they are inspired by modernist architecture and minimal art.

Ariadne Kapelioti Thessaloniki, Greece > p. 164
hello@superlora.com | www.superlora.com
Although her background is in physics, Ariadne Kapelioti subsequently turned to the world of jewellery and fashion design, founding Superlora, the first 3D printed jewellery brand in Greece. Superlora's jewellery offers an innovative approach to contemporary design, and its pieces are intended to be an extension of the wearer. This chunky jewellery's attention to detail, precision and experimentation are made possible through advanced digital technology and flawless craftsmanship, and each piece has a sophisticated and vibrant twist. The careful designs of Superlora's Future02 collection turn Euclidean circle theorems into patterns and forms of wearable art.

Artemis Valsamaki Athens,Greece > p. 202-203
es.miarte@yahoo.gr | www.artemisvalsamaki.com
Artemis was born in Athens, Greece, where she completed her studies, graduating initially as a graphic designer and later as a silversmith specialized in handmade jewellery. For Artemis, jewellery is a medium for manifesting thoughts and concerns as well as for expressing feelings. She draws her inspiration from human relationships, dreams, Greek mythology, reality, fantasy and anything that hides an emotional power. She always aims to create a visual narrative story that can be worn.

Aurélie Guillaume Montréal, Canada/Residing in Chicago, IL, USA > p. 84-85
www.aurelieguillaume.com
Aurélie Guillaume trained in the arts of jewellery and metalsmithing at the École de Joaillerie de Montréal and at NSCAD University in Canada. Her pieces have been acquired for the permanent collections of the Enamel Arts Foundation in Los Angeles and the Museum of Art and Design in New York. Using the traditional technique of cloisonné enamelling, she is reviving the idea of narrative in enamelling in a contemporary context, fuelled by street art, comics, pop art and counterculture. Her illustrations transcend the two-dimensional realm of paper and are given new life in the physical world as wearable objects.

>> B >>

Babette von Dohnanyi Hamburg, Germany > p. 72
info@babettevdohnanyi.com | www.babettevdohnanyi.com
To design jewelery means a never ending fascination. To find new forms for the combination of color and material, to invent at the same time elegant and yet provocative solutions is the great challenge in this process. To achieve an optimal technical solution forthis aesthetic aim in each individual piece I consider therefore as the core of my work. The history of jewellery art shows that geometric form and lithe portability of a jewellery piece should be not a contradiction .this is an important view of my jewellery work.
...they maintained that shade is a part of light. It sounds absurd when I express it; but so it is: for they said that colours, which are shadow and the result of shade,are light itself. – Johann Eckermann,Conversations of Goethe

Barbara Paganin Venice, Italy > p. 142-143
paganinb@hotmail.com
Barbara Paganin was born in Venice in 1961, and her pieces can be found in many important museums worldwide. In her jewellery designs, precious metals are accompanied by porcelains, acrylic resins and Venetian glass beads, as well as by small objects and antique portraits. She sees the world as a vast field of sensory research. She investigates the principles of universe and society by observing the simplest life forms and the most common objects. Her experiences are therefore closely connected with her art and vice versa. Through a continuous narrative process, she weaves her thick net of information via a sort of genetic algorithm in which everyone can find a reflection and a precise reference.

Biba Schutz New York, NY, USA > p. 216
bibaschutz@gmail.com | www.bibaschutz.
Biba Schutz is a self-taught studio jeweller from New York City who holds a degree in design. Her jewellery is an evolution of her personal relationship with materials, processes and emotion. She has been published in Metalsmith Magazine, American Craft Magazine, New Glass Review, Lark Books's 500 series, books from Promopress Editions and publications by the AJF. Recently, she co-curated the "Shadow Themes" exhibition at Gallery RR in New York. In 2016, she was selected to participate in Schmuck. Her studio practice is supported by national and international group and solo gallery shows and fairs, and her pieces have been acquired by museums and private collectors.

>> C >>

Camilla Luihn Oslo, Norway > p. 156-157, 212
camilla.luihn@gmail.com | www.luihn.no
Camilla Luihn obtained a master of arts from the Oslo National Academy of the Arts in 1994. She has exhibited her pieces at a number of exhibitions in Norway and outside her home country. Her artistic practices include jewellery, photography, design and graphic prints. Her combining of technical expertise and an awareness of objects' function enables her to create pieces with poetic elements that are presented through different thematic projects. Camilla moves in a landscape where she walks the thin line between the intimate and "regular" on one side and the spectacular and unusual on the other. Her approach to enamelling creates a reminiscence of a visual aesthetic that is not obvious and present immediately but exists as an unconscious echo of an experience or memories.

Carolina Bernachea Buenos Aires, Argentina > p. 43, 46
info@carolinabernachea.com | www.carolinabernachea.com
Determination, meticulousness, patience, research, calculation processes and academic training have all had an unconscious influence on Carolina Bernachea's particular working methodology. She is intrigued by the transformations that materials undergo and by the sensations that she feels at each stage of change. Concebida explores contemporary textile arts, merging them with traditional techniques. Everything comes together in her manually woven and dyed pieces, which emphasize the nobility of natural materials and can be worn or used as decoration pieces. Lo inesperado de lo cotidiano describes a walk through the city and those indiscreet traces that are left at random: confusion, laughter, phobias, or good-luck wishes.

Céline Sylvestre Annecy, France / Residing in Paris, France > p. 182
celinesylvestre.l@gmail.com | www.celinesylvestre.com
After completing a goldsmithing apprenticeship in Lyon, Céline Sylvestre trained in contemporary jewellery, and in 2003 she obtained her diploma from the AFEDAP School of Applied Arts in Paris. Since then, she has been creating unique jewellery pieces that question our relationship with time and the memory of our bodies. Although her work has moved away from classical jewellery and embraced a conceptual approach, she remains devoted to metalworking and has trained in rare techniques. She was a laureate at Villa Kujoyama in 2015; this residency allowed her to spend five months in Japan and continues to inspire her works. Since 2011, she has been part of the D'un bijou to the other association.

Chao-Hsien Kuo Tainan, Taiwan / Residing in Lahti, Finland > p. 21
chao@chaoeero.com | www.chao-hsienkuo.com
Chao-Hsien Kuo holds a bachelor's degree in fine arts from Hofstra University in the United States and a master's degree in industrial design from Aalto University in Finland. She also completed a two-year postgraduate programme at the Lahti Institute of Design's School of Goldsmithing. She currently co-manages a contemporary jewellery brand, Chao & Eero, and designs collections for Lapponia Jewelry. Chao-Hsien has been exhibiting her jewellery around the world since the late 1990s. Her works have a very recognizable style, and they often reflect her appreciation of the natural surroundings in Finland.

Charity Hall Los Angeles, California / Residing in Blacksburg, VA, USA > p. 22-23
charityhall@yahoo.com | charityhall.com
Charity Hall received a BA in biology from Colorado College in 2000 and an MFA in metal design from East Carolina University in 2008. Her enamels have been acquired for the Enamel Arts Foundation's collection. In her own words, "My work illustrates a diverse array of insects to increase awareness and appreciation for entomological life. Anthropomorphically biased, we focus only on the exasperations specific to the human condition – the blood-thirsty mosquito, the menacing cockroach lurking beneath the kitchen stove. So ready to smack, squish and spray, we fail to appreciate the evolutionary aptitude and anatomical brilliance of these savage bugs. From intricate venation patterns within glassy amber wings to microscopically formidable tarsi, complex microcosms of line, form and texture abound."

Christine Jalio Helsinki, Finland / Residing in Lapua, Finland > p. 200
christine.jalio@gmail.com | www.christinejalio.fi
Christine Jalio is a thirty-eight-year-old jewellery artist from Finland. She is fascinated by old and worn elements, roughness and decay. Her Past, Loss, Future collection shows that she is intrigued by asceticism, old age and sensitivity. The collection tells the story of aging and personal loss and of the human life span and its transitions, choices and turning points. After finishing degrees in both metal arts and silversmithing, she completed a bachelor's degree in jewellery design at Lahti University. She expresses herself by making contemporary jewellery that often reflects her fascination with the human psyche and the emotions and reactions that are part of it.

Christoph Straube Munich, Germany / Residing in Nuremberg, Germany > p. 219
mail@christoph-straube.de | christoph-straube.de
Christoph's jewellery pieces are reminiscent of geometric watercolour drawings as a result of their finely painted black enamel lines and shadings on a white background coating. The white background serves as a canvas, on which an illusionary three-dimensional space is created through the drafted perspective. Traces from the working process such as slight colour changes and enamel dust are left deliberately to allow each piece to maintain its hand-drawn character. Overlapping parts play with a three-dimensionality that lies between the drawing and the real object.

Cova Ríos Madrid, Spain > p. 131
covarios@covarios.com | www.covarios.com
Cova holds a doctorate in architecture from Madrid's School of Architecture and the Milan Polytechnic, and he is also qualified as a technical specialist in design and artistic jewellery. Since 1998, he has been collaborating with architecture and design firms, an activity that he combines with teaching; presenting work at numerous painting, sculpture and jewellery exhibitions; and participating in national and international fairs. His architectural and artistic training gives him a grasp of all art-related disciplines and limitless freedom in his use of materials and techniques. As a result, he is able to produce creations with total freedom without being confined to a specific field. His work therefore encompasses architecture, paintings, jewellery, site specifics and design.

Cristina Zani Italy / Residing in Edinburgh, UK > p. 126, 144
info@cristinazani.com | www.cristinazani.com
Following a career in corporate communication, Italian-born artist Cristina Zani completed her MFA in jewellery at Edinburgh College of Art in June 2012. In 2011, she was awarded a bursary that enabled her to study jewellery in Seoul for four months. After living and working in several countries, Cristina is now based in Edinburgh. Her present work is influenced by the urban landscape and inspired by Calvino's Invisible Cities. She approaches the creation of her jewellery in the same way that one would compose a story, and like Marco Polo in Invisible Cities, she borrows elements from the city's landscape to visually describe it and subtly suggest it to the viewer.

Curtis H. Arima Berkeley, CA, USA > p. 170
curtis@curtisharima.com | www.curtisharima.com
Curtis H. Arima is an associate professor and a cochair of the jewellery and metal arts programme at California College of the Arts. He produces jewellery and sculpture in his Berkeley studio. His work has been exhibited across the country and abroad, including at SOFA NY and Chicago, the National Ornamental Museum in Memphis, and Vennel Gallery in Scotland. His awards include Best of Show at the Innovations in Contemporary Craft exhibition in Richmond, CA, and he has been nominated for Instructor of the Year for the Niche Awards. His publications include Metalsmith magazine, Sculpture magazine and the Lark's 500 Series. He received a BFA from CCAC and an MFA in metalsmithing from Cranbrook Academy of Art.

>> D >>

Dauvit Alexander – The Justified Sinner Scotland / Residing in Birmingham, UK > p. 74-75
www.justified-sinner.com
Dauvit Alexander, The Justified Sinner, has been making jewellery since he was fourteen. Although trained as a fine jeweller, he has become well known in contemporary jewellery circles for his work using found objects and materials, especially corroded iron from industrial wastelands. His work treats this material as precious, and he uses his craft skills to combine it with the more traditional materials of jewellery. His most recent work has been more pared back, allowing the corroded iron to speak for itself in a bold series of pieces that characterize the collapse of Europe's industrial heartlands.

Donald Friedlich Montclair, NJ, USA / Residing in Madison, WI, USA > p. 222
dfriedlich@aol.com | www.donaldfriedlich.com
Donald Friedlich received his BFA from RISD in 1982. He served a term as president of the Society of North American Goldsmiths. His jewellery is in the permanent collections of the Victoria and Albert Museum, the Smithsonian American Art Museum, the Museum of Fine Arts Boston, the Cooper Hewitt Design Museum and the Schmuckmuseum, among many others. Donald's Aqua Series jewellery is inspired by rippling wave patterns in water. His recent Organic Series designs, cast from apples, asparagus, celery and other foods, are a major departure from his primarily abstract history. His hope is that transforming such prosaic and ephemeral materials into wearable glass allows the wearer to see the beauty and elegance of their forms in a new light.

Dongyi Wu Bengbu, China / Residing in Rochester, NY, USA > p. 30
dongyiwu.jewelry@gmail.com | www.dongyiwu.com
Dongyi Wu was born and raised in Bengbu and then moved to Xiamen, China. She completed her undergraduate studies at the Beijing Institute of Fashion Technology, where she majored in jewellery art design. She then continued her artistic explorations at Rochester Institute of Technology. She is now a studio resident in both the fine arts jewellery design and sculpture programs at RIT. Her artworks tend to describe silent or mysterious dreamlands. She uses simple and abstract but organic techniques to depict narrative stories in her pieces. She has also created new materials with unique textures, and these have become one of the essential features of her art. Her pieces continue to be exhibited at galleries, fashion weeks and conferences.

Dot > p. 33, 102
dotmelanin@gmail.com
I find my way in silence / there is no right and wrong / no explanations or excuses / I close my eyes and go with the flow / what I do today will not come tomorrow / there is no "material," there is freedom / environment / meeting point of imagination and I'm the crossroad / author of worlds.

>> E >>

Edna Madera Melrose Park, IL, USA / Residing in Kansas City, MO, USA > p. 118
emt@ednamadera.com | www.ednamadera.com
Edna Madera earned a BFA in metalsmithing from Southern Illinois University Carbondale in 2001. She then completed an MFA, also in metalsmithing, at the Rochester Institute of Technology in 2004. Since completing her academic studies, Edna has worked in various roles in the jewellery industry for over a decade. She started out as a bench jeweller, performing fine jewellery repair and stone setting, before then working as a jewellery designer, bringing to life silver designs produced on a mass scale. She currently works as a product development manager for a jewellery and keepsakes company. She also remains active in the studio and exhibits her work at American craft shows.

Edu Tarin Valencia, Spain / Residing in Idar-Oberstein, Germany > p. 218
contact@edutarin.com | www.edutarin.com
Edu's parents were jewellers, and so he learned his skills in the family business. In 2008, he began studying jewellery at EASD in Valencia, and he continued his bachelor's and master's studies in Idar-Oberstein, Germany. Since 2010, he has participated in different exhibitions throughout Europe, and his work has been recognized through prestigious international awards. In his own words, "I create a singular place. It is in silence that we can hear the sound of a being, leading me to establish the limits of its structure. I evoke the interior and give it presence, and I turn nothingness into material and emptiness into content."

Elin Flognman Örebro, Sweden / Residing in Trollhättan, Sweden > p. 99
flognman@mail.nu | www.elinflognman.com
Elin resides in an old factory town on the west coast of Sweden. She takes an interest in our desire to escape everyday life. Her artistic ambition is to find the point of intersection between the familiar and the extraordinary – for example, when a person repeats his or her name over and over again until it begins to sound strange. Basic activities such as walking and eating permeate her work, and walking is her source of inspiration. By listening to everyday objects, she seeks to make every day matter.

Emily Cobb Philadelphia, PA, USA / Residing in California, USA > p. 172-173
studio@emily-cobb.com | www.emily-cobb.com
Emily Cobb is a jewellery designer and maker from Philadelphia who utilizes 3D printing technology and traditional jewellery-making techniques to create her work. She received her MFA in metals, jewellery and CAD-CAM from Tyler School of Art, and she is an assistant professor at Humboldt State University in California. Her work has been featured on the cover of Metalsmith Magazine, and she has exhibited at museums such as the Racine Art Museum and the Bellevue Arts Museum. By imagining another reality in which animals show signs of aging in unusual ways, Emily explores both the appealing and destructive results of this process.

Emily Pellini Kennett Square, PA, USA / Residing in Lancaster, PA, USA > p. 88
pellini.emily.a@gmail.com
Emily Pellini graduated from Millersville University with a BFA in studio arts, within which she focused on fine art metals and jewellery. She was the Emerging Artist in Residence for Millersville the following year. Her work is a combination of symbolism and narrative, mixed with some personal iconography. The character in her Swarming Brooch series is original and part of an ongoing narrative about addiction, from discovery to rock bottom.

Emily Watson Chapel Hill, NC, USA / Residing in Rochester, NY, USA > p. 51
mail1@metalemily.com | www.metalemily.com
Emily has been showing her works in the United States and internationally for almost fifteen years. Her current work focuses on mimicry and artificiality, using mostly manmade materials that resemble elements of the natural world. Her hand-carved brooches blend modern materials with vintage ones. When making brooches, she frequently returns to imagery of birds and their habitat.

Erica Bello Baltimore, MD, USA > p. 169
ericabellojewelry@gmail.com | www.ericabellojewelry.com
Erica Bello studied metals and jewellery design at the Rochester Institute of Technology's School for American Crafts, from which she received her BFA. She currently resides in Baltimore, MD, and works out of her studio located in the Station North Arts District. Influenced by icons of value and strength, Erica's work communicates an interest in the reduction of powerful imagery. Through her use of traditional fabrication techniques, minimal forms are crafted as intersecting planes or with exposed interiors. The hollowness and skeletal nature of these objects are amplified through the use of monochromatic industrial finishes.

Estela Saez Vilanova Girona, Spain / Residing in Barcelona, Spain > p. 183
info@estelasaez.com | www.estelasaez.com
A Catalan maker and educator, Estela's oeuvre spans the past twenty years. Her jewellery derives its evocative power from its distance from the ground rather than from its distance from the skin. Yet while her pieces are sculptural, the shapes that she uses are proportionate to the hand: Estela belongs to a relatively small group of makers whose practice is guided by the dual sculptural and wearable nature of contemporary jewellery. Educated at the Massana School in Barcelona, she received the Massana Award in 2001. She subsequently worked as a studio assistant to Professor Ruudt Peters. In 2006, she won Munich's Talente Prize. She also holds a master of arts from Trier University, Idar-Oberstein.

Eunseon Park South Korea / Residing in Halifax, Canada > p. 136
eunseonpark44@gmail.com
Eunseon Park is a Korean jeweller and metalsmith who is based in Halifax, Canada. She completed a BFA at NSCAD University in 2017, majoring in jewellery design and metalsmithing. Eunseon's intention is to imbue her pieces with her personal impression of nature. She is immersed in visualizing the strength as well as the delicacy of flowers and plants using sheet metals. With her method of shearing the edge of a thin metal sheet as a forming process, she experiences the unrestrained beauty of metals, and the process echoes how she feels about nature. Another major factor in her working process is her use of and experimentation with diverse methods for applying colour to metal.

Eva Burton Buenos Aires, Argentina / Residing in Idar-Oberstein, Germany > p. 127
evaburtonjoyas@gmail.com | www.evaburtonjoyasdeautor.blogspot.com
Eva Burton is a jewellery maker who lives and works in Idar-Oberstein, Germany. She was born in Buenos Aires, Argentina, where she studied art restoration at the University of Fine Arts. In 2014, she graduated from Professor Ramón Puig Cuyás's class at the Escola Massana in Barcelona. Since 2015, she has been completing an MFA at the University of Applied Sciences Trier. She is always seeking new methods of expression, and playing is a fundamental aspect of her life and her artistic creations.

Eva Fernandez Martos Spain / Residing in Nottingham, UK > p. 47
zoemfdez@hotmail.com | www.evafernandezmartos.co.uk
I am a mechanical engineer retrained as a jewellery designer living in the UK. I recently graduated with a Masters of Fine Art in Jewellery Design from Edinburgh College of Art. I continue developing my practice as a designer/maker in parallel with teaching metalwork and digital design at Nottingham Trent University.
We live surrounded by an overflowing man-made world of objects which pass fleetingly through our lives without acknowledgement. With my work, I help people appreciate the ordinary and our man-made surroundings by stimulating their curiosity and perception. I achieve this by taking inspiration from our manufactured environment and move ordinary objects (or features of them) out of their usual contexts or configurations to portray social and political matters.

Evgeniia Balashova Murmansk, Russia / Residing in Glasgow, Scotland > p. 165
evebalashova@gmail.com | www.evebalashova.com
The inspiration for Evgeniia's work originates from office spaces and the abundance of repetitive features found within them – for example, stationery, computer hardware and furniture. These elements all appear in perfect order until human intervention turns them into organized chaos. Evgeniia explores this curious relationship through a combination of contrasts. Through the use of 3D printing and traditional handicraft skills, she creates a balance between soft, flowing curves and strict geometrical precision. She uses the cube, a reference to an office cubicle, as a basis for many of her pieces. This acts as a starting point for transforming a basic shape into a vibrant, energetic object.

Ezra Satok-Wolman Toronto, Canada / Residing in Ontario, Canada > p. 83, 176
esw@atelierhg.com | www.atelierhg.com
For Ezra, creating jewellery is a process of discovery that involves research and experimentation, in terms of both concept and material. He uses geometry as a language to generate visual representations of his ideas and philosophies about the universe and our place within it. The constants that are present in his work are universal and are used to draw parallels between microcosm and macrocosm.

>> F >>

Felieke van der Leest Emmen, The Netherlands / Residing in Øystese, Norway > p. 92-93, 168
felieke@feliekevanderleest.com | www.feliekevanderleest.com
Felieke van der Leest is a trained metalsmith who graduated from the jewellery department at the Rietveld Academie, Netherlands, in 1996. Her passion for animals started in her childhood, as did her love for crocheting. By combining this technique with precious metals and plastic toy animals, she has developed her own idiom for contemporary jewellery and art objects.

Fernanda Mitsue Brazil > p. 186
fernandamitsue@gmail.com
Fascinated by the endless creative possibilities that sculptural forms allow, Fernanda Mitsue found in jewellery the ideal field in which to express herself. She began her studies in traditional jewellery in 2011, and between 2013 and 2015 she studied artistic jewellery in Madrid. Since then, she has focused on creating pieces that convey calm and balance. Her works are always strongly influenced by the art of her Japanese ancestors. She uses jewellery as an artistic medium, and so brooches are her favourite form when she is creating.

Ferràn Iglesias Barón Terrassa, Catalonia, Spain / Residing in Matadepera, Catalonia, Spain > p. 66
ferraiglesiasbaron@gmail.com | ferraniglesiasbaron@weebly.com
A Spanish artist and jewellery maker, Ferràn Iglesias Barón has over twenty years of goldsmithing experience that encompasses academic studies and written publications, teaching experience, exhibitions, and the receipt of numerous awards. Essence and meaning are the two driving forces of his growth and creative process, and he explores them in nature and through geometry or colour. For Ferràn, interacting with different mediums and chromas expresses emotion and transcends aesthetics to create a new form of beauty and appeal, a subtle sentiment of contentment, or what one might call happiness.

Florencia Alonso Buenos Aires, Argentina > p. 130
floraretes@hotmail.com | Instagram: @florecen
Where obscurity is to be found, Florencia Alonso likes to observe hidden beauty: abandoned wood at construction sites, cotton balls that seek to be spun into new threads, newspapers that describe yesterday's stories, pine seeds strewn on the streets of Buenos Aires, or bags of rubbish that always seem ready to be imminently moved. She works with appearances, creating and constructing with materials while playing with the characteristics that they seem to possess but in fact do not. She likes to reinvent their journeys and to give them new meanings and new stories to tell so that they have new destinations and become questions.

>> G >>

Gabriele Hinze Essen, Germany / Residing in Berlin, Germany > p. 35, 146
hinze.gabriele@outlook.de
Gabriele Hinze was born in 1964 in Essen, and she began her career by completing a goldsmithing apprenticeship and then working as a goldsmith. In 1990, she participated in the Summer Academy in Salzburg with Johanna Dahm. She studied at Düsseldorf University of Applied Sciences and has been a freelancer since 1995. In 1996, she was one of the founding members of the Elft group of designers. She was a member of the SchmuckProdukt group in Essen between 1998 and 2003, and she was coproprietor of the gallery of the same name. From 2005 until 2008, she lectured at Düsseldorf University of Applied Sciences. She has lived and worked in Berlin since 2008.

Georg W. Dobler Creussen, Germany / Residing in Berlin and Halle, Germany > p. 38
georg.dobler@hawk-hhg.de
Georg W. Dobler is trained as a goldsmith, and he obtained his master's degree in 1980. From 1974 until 1980, he was involved in designing and manufacturing classic jewellery. Since 1980, he has worked as a freelancer and jewellery artist with his own studio. He has been teaching all over the world since 1987, and since 2002 he has been professor of jewellery at HAWK University of Applied Arts and Sciences in Hildesheim, Germany.

Gerti Machacek Vienna, Austria > p. 117
gerti.machacek@atelier-machacek.at | www.atelier-machacek.at | www.animavienna.com
Gerti's work has been widely published and exhibited both nationally and internationally. In 1992, she was awarded the Austrian State Crafts Prize. Her pieces are held in collections at the MAK and the Artothek in Vienna, as well as in the Bollmann and Basiner Collections and in several other private collections. Her work is characterized by the playful manner in which she handles body and form. Ideas and design considerations determine her choice of materials and techniques. She places emphasis on sculptural pieces that can also serve as mementos or objects that encourage self-identification. Through its portability and innate movement, her jewellery produces shifts in perspective.

Gésine Hackenberg Mainz, Germany / Residing in Amsterdam, The Netherlands > p. 152, 206-207
mail@gesinehackenberg.com | www.gesinehackenberg.com
Gésine Hackenberg is an Amsterdam-based artist who uses diverse techniques to explore the conceptual intersections between jewellery and objects from everyday life. She was trained as a goldsmith in Germany and graduated in 2001 from the Gerrit Rietveld Academie in Amsterdam. In 2013, she earned her MA from the PXL-MAD School of Arts in Hasselt, Belgium, where she is currently teaching. Gésine has received several grants and awards over the course of her career. Her work is included in various public collections such as those of the Stedelijk Museum Amsterdam, the Victoria and Albert Museum in London and the MAD in New York City.

Gigi Mariani Modena, Italy > p. 163
gigimarianimo@virgilio.it | info@gigimariani.it | www.gigimariani.it
Gigi is a goldsmith from Modena who has over thirty years of jewellery-making experience, having opened his studio in Modena in 1985. His conceptual jewellery has been exhibited in prestigious group exhibitions worldwide as well as in galleries in Rome, Luxembourg, Munich, Vienna and Riga. His goal is to move from the concept of simple jewellery to a larger concept of sculpture and artwork. He utilizes antique and unique goldsmithing techniques such as niello. He works with precious metals, combining them with other metals such as iron, copper and brass. Just as a painter uses a canvas for self-expression, Gigi uses his jewellery as a basis for conveying his feelings.

Giovanna Canu – Joy Jo Sassari, Sardinia, Italy / Residing in Milan, Italy > p. 90
info@joy-jo.it | www.joy-jo.it
For Giovanna, rediscovering weaving, a technique she first encountered when she was still a child, was like rediscovering a thread that has run throughout her life. After a long career as an architect and designer, she decided to make a fresh start and embark upon a road paved with study, research and experimentation. She developed a passion for textile jewellery and, crucially, a love for metal. Whether the metal in question is cold or hot, matte or glossy, rigid or pliable, expensive or cheap, she sees it as a loyal friend with the capacity to give physical form to her thought. The force of her fingers, the ductility of the material and the intensity of her soul all work together to express and share her emotions.

Gregory Larin Tula, Russia / Residing in Tel Aviv, Israel > p. 103
gritzel@gmail.com | www.gregory-larin.com
Gregory Larin was born in Tula, a Russian industrial city known for manufacturing weapons and gingerbread. After immigrating at the age of nineteen to Israel in 1997, he joined the IDF, where he served as an aircraft builder with the air force for two and a half years. This was where he discovered his creativity, and once his military service ended, he took a government-funded metalworking course. He then decided to explore this field within the academic world. In 2007, he graduated with honours from the department of jewellery design at the prestigious Shenkar College of Engineering and Design. Since then, his work has been exhibited around the world.

>> H >>

Hadas Levin Tel-Aviv, Israel > p. 118
levinhadas@gmail.com | hadaslevin.com
Hadas Levin's Road Marks series is made with a sintering process that uses black steel metal powders. The marks that embedded into the material are primal and unique. Firing at a very high temperature brings the product to its final stage. The binding adhesives are burned away and the metal particles are sintered to create the final metal object. The technique enables hollow-form objects made of steel to be created as one block, without soldering or any other form of adhesives or joints. A bit like a voyage in time, this approach brings together current high-tech materials and traditional low-tech crafting techniques.

Hannah-May Chapman London, UK / Residing in Brighton, UK > p. 100
info@hannahmaychapman.com | www.hannahmaychapman.com
Hidden depth and meaning can be found in most things these days, but Hannah-May Chapman chooses to hide nothing in her jewellery and aims to entertain and put a smile on people's faces. Over the years and alongside her studies in theatre arts and jewellery, she has worked as an aircraft broker, a gallery assistant, a publisher's foreign-rights assistant and even a domestic cleaner. Despite gaining a mass of experience, her passion for creating jewellery has remained her focus. Because she has seen the world through many different sets of "eyes", her approach to making is always playful. She uses bright colours, a combination of obvious and abstract forms, and a variety of materials that let her sense of humour speak through her work.

Hedvig Westermark Stockholm, Sweden > p. 67, 205
hedvig.westermark@gmail.com | www.smideochform.se
Hedvig Westermark has been running a studio for over thirty years, and she has always thought that making and wearing jewellery is the perfect way to communicate. Whether she is making concept-based pieces for an exhibition or crafting a piece for a particular individual, for Hedvig, creating jewellery is a way to tell a story about something or somebody and to make a statement that may be political, religious, private or just provocative. Putting all the parts that go in to making a jewellery piece together is in Hedvig's opinion similar to putting letters together to form a word, then putting the words together to make a sentence, then putting sentences together. Or, to put it another way, placing a piece of jewellery on your body makes you ready to communicate!

Heidemarie Herb Germany / Residing in Italy > p. 31
heidemarie.herb@gmail.com | www.heidemarieherb.com
After qualifying as a goldsmith in Germany in 1991, Heidemarie Herb received a certificate in precious gems at the German Diamond Institute (DDI). Her works have been displayed in a number of prominent exhibitions in more than fifteen countries. She has been the recipient of awards in Poland, Russia and Italy. Her works are held at the Museum of Amber and at Malbork Castle Museum in Poland and at the Cominelli Foundation in Italy, as well as in private collections in Austria, the United States and Lithuania. Movements, forms, lightness and colours in harmony with each other are important in each of her works, which she likes to use to preserve memories and thoughts.

Helen Habtay Idar-Oberstein, Germany > p. 210

hhabtay@hotmail.de | www.apparat.be/artist/helen-habtay

Helen Habtay is a jewellery maker from Germany with roots in Eritrea. She graduated with a bachelor's degree in jewellery and accessories from Middlesex University, London, in 2013. Since 2014, she has been studying on the MFA programme at Trier University of Applied Sciences in Idar-Oberstein, Germany. In her work, Helen addresses the merging of adornment and body. She creates sculptural jewellery born out of geometric forms and made from readymades, leather and hand-carved gemstones. The driving force behind her work is a continuous inquisitiveness about the relationship between body and adornment, underpinned by what objects mean to us in society.

Helmi Lindblom Finland > p. 91

info@strangebutjewelry.com www.strangebutjewelry.com

Helmi graduated from Lahti Institute of Design and Fine Arts in 2015. She holds a BA in culture and arts and is a goldsmithing artisan. Her work is a dialogue between different tactile surfaces and colours that creates a playful body, titillating the eye but speaking directly to the fingertips. As she puts it, "I pay attention to my surrounding world, especially things and happenings that trigger childlike joy. Playfulness is a place where I want the person to stop. I think that the power of playing charges our batteries over and over again; one just has to learn to indulge in it."

Heng Lee Kaohsiung, Taiwan > p. 52-53

henglee1017@msn.com | www.facebook.com/HengLeeJewelry

Through making jewellery, Heng Lee expresses the inspiration that he derives from the luxurious costumes and jewellery found in Eastern and Western history. Traditional Chinese crafts are another inspiration in his work, and he believes that mixing traditional patterns with contemporary jewellery produces a creative spark. In his series of works, he uses enlarged images of decorative elements, and as a result of this magnifying process, some pixels of the pattern are blurred, producing a mosaic effect.

Hind ElHafez Cairo, Egypt > p. 166

hind.elhafez@cairoartistscollective.com | www.cairoartistscollective.com

After completing a degree in architecture at Cairo University, Hind studied art at St. Martin's in London and at the Art Students League of New York. She also trained under the mentorship of Magd El Siginy in Cairo. She has been making and selling her own line of jewellery since 2001. Hind is passionate about the process of designing and creating contemporary jewellery. She is a member of the Cairo Artists Collective.

>> I >>

Ignasi Cavaller Triay Menorca, Spain / Residing in Barcelona, Spain > p. 54

ignasicavaller@gmail.com | www.ignasicavaller.com

Ignasi's first contact with jewellery was at the age of sixteen at the Escola d'Arts i Oficis de Menorca. Four years later, he moved to Barcelona to study at the Escola Massana, where he discovered the art form of jewellery. He continued his training at the South Carelia Polytechnic University in Finland, and in 2012 he moved to Idar-Oberstein, Germany, to study at the Hochschule Trier, where he obtained his MFA in 2015. He spent 2016 teaching at Azza Fahmy Studio in Cairo. And now he's back in Barcelona, continuing his work and creating new pieces.

Iris Merkle Stuttgart, Germany > p. 41

mail@iris-merkle.de | www.iris-merkle.de

Iris Merkle has lived and worked in Stuttgart, southern Germany, for more than ten years. She studied jewellery design at Pforzheim's renowned School of Design and also at the University of Art and Design in Helsinki, Finland. She has run her own studio since 2007 and holds exhibitions at home and abroad. Her works have been awarded with prizes such as the 2014 Design Art Craft award from the German state of Baden-Württemberg and the GEDOK FormART-Prize in 2017. In 2015, she presented her works in New York at the annual contemporary jewellery exhibition at the MAD.

Isabelle Busnell Tonnerre, France/Residing in London, UK > p. 213

busnelisabelle@gmail.com | www.isabellebusnel.co.uk

After a fifteen-year career in finance and banking, an urge to express herself in a different way led Isabelle Busnell to retrain. She obtained a diploma in jewellery in 2008 and a research MA in 2010, both from the Sir John Cass Department of Art, Media and Design at London Metropolitan University. Her work explores the stereotypes of classic jewellery and gives them a contemporary twist by turning them into magnetic silicone-rubber brooches. In Isabelle's view, silicone rubber is a fascinating material for jewellery that, when appropriately worked, lures viewers into mistaking it for ceramic, plaster or even glass. People are drawn in to grabbing and touching her pieces, only to realise that they are not what they initially thought they were, a quality that makes her works visually intriguing and socially communicative.

>> J >>

Jaki Coffey Cork, Ireland / Residing in Dublin, Ireland > p. 96

jakicoffey@gmail.com | www.jakicoffey.com

Jaki Coffey is an award-winning Dublin-based designer and maker from Cork, Ireland. She holds an MFA in design from the National College of Art and Design, Dublin. Her jewellery comprises personal narratives translated into colourful, playful, interactive pieces. Wearers of her works are encouraged to play and fidget with them. She achieves her intentions with attentive design, humour and careful consideration of the materials that she uses, which range from precious metals to found objects. Her work has been shown around Europe, including at Ireland's National Craft Gallery and Schmuck.

James Dunn Wheaton, IL, USA / Residing in Edinboro, PA, USA > p. 154-155

james.dunn90@icloud.com | jamesdunnmetals.com

James Dunn received his bachelor's degree from The University of Wisconsin – La Crosse in 2013 and his MFA from Edinboro University of Pennsylvania in 2017. He describes his creative process as follows: "Much of our world is made up of manufactured objects, void of the human imprint. We become blind to these objects because of their uniformity and repetition. I extract these objects from their cold, stark environments and warm them through contact with the body. I am interested in how mass-produced, utilitarian objects transform when they are recreated at an intimate size and placed on the body. I am interested in how the objects change but also how the wearer changes. How can wearing jewellery transform a person's perception of their environment?"

Jan Smith Canada > p. 122

jansmithca@hotmail.com | www.jansmith.ca

Jan Smith holds a BFA from Canada's NSCAD University. Her work has been included in publications such as On Body and Soul, Contemporary Armour and Amulets, the 500 Series by Lark, Color on Metal and Signs of Life 2008. Galerie Noel Guyomarc'h, Velvet Da Vinci and Facere Jewelry Art Gallery represent Smith's work. According to Jan, "My work evolves from an intimate connection to place and reflects a deep sense of knowing that place. The mark making, comprising repetitive lines and dots, references surfaces and textures from my environment. The work commemorates fleeting moments of sensory pleasure within our lives."

János Gábor Varga Campo Ligure, Genoa, Italy > p. 180

blindspotjewellery@gmail.com | blindspotjewellery.com

János Gábor Varga first studied agriculture in his native Hungary, where he carried out ethnoveterinary research for ten years. He started making jewellery after moving to England. Aside from a basic-level course, he is largely self-taught. Now living in Italy, he runs his own workshop in a village near Genoa. János is inspired by metal tools and the natural textures created by their use. He constantly experiments with all sorts of materials, although his favourite is iron.

Jeanne Marell Huissen, The Netherlands / Residing in Copenhagen, Denmark, and London, UK > p. 36

www.jeannemarell.com

Jeanne Marell designs and makes minimalist jewellery with a twist from her studios in London and Copenhagen, whilst working as a renowned product and service designer in her "other life". She counts Cadillac, HP, Nokia and Samsung among her clients. In the last few years, she has ventured into the world of jewellery, designing and making pieces to high acclaim. There is an undeniable fascination with geometry and construction throughout Jeanne's oeuvre. This passion for geometry is reflected in the Spirograph collection, which harks back to childhood Spirograph drawings. Jeanne builds complicated, geometric nylon-wire constructions fixed into various precious-metal frames. In a similar manner to an optical illusion, the rhythmic nature of these patterns draws one in.

Jeffrey Lloyd Dever Laurel, MD, USA > p. 68
jeff@deverdesigns.com | jeffreylloyddever.com
Trained as a graphic designer, Jeffrey Lloyd Dever has worked and taught design, illustration, and jewellery techniques for over twenty years. His work resides in numerous museums and private collections. All of his jewellery pieces are miniature sculptural studies. The fact that they are wearable at all is almost incidental to the poetic qualities that he seeks. Each piece is born through a series of sketches, which mature into fabricated forms of polymer clay built over reinforced armatures. Through repeated cycles of fabrication, veneering and oven curing, his pieces grow layer by layer. Each colour gradient is the actual colour of the clay, and one of his pieces can easily go through ten to twenty fabrication/curing cycles and take weeks to complete.

Jessica Calderwood Ohio, USA / Residing in Indiana, USA > p. 94-95
jc1010@hotmail.com | jcalderwood@bsu.edu | www.jessicacalderwood.com
Jessica Calderwood is an image maker and sculptor who works in esoteric craft media. She uses a combination of traditional and industrial metalworking processes as a means to make statements about contemporary life. She received her BFA from the Cleveland Institute of Art and her MFA, which involved an emphasis on metalworking, from Arizona State University. She has exhibited throughout the United States and internationally at curated and juried exhibitions. She has participated in artist residencies with the John Michael Kohler Arts/Industry Program, Ferro Corporation, and the Mesa Arts Center. Her work has also been published in Metalsmith Magazine, American Craft, NICHE, Ornament, the Lark 500 series and The Art of Enameling. She is currently an associate professor of art at Ball State University.

Jo Pond London, UK / Residing in Staffordshire, UK > p. 165
jo@jopond.com | www.jopond.com
Jo Pond is based in rural Staffordshire in England. She earned her master's degree at the Birmingham School of Jewellery, where she now serves as a part-time lecturer alongside her studio practice. Her work has been exhibited on an international platform; highlights include Schmuck 2007 and 2014 (Munich), the V&A Museum (London), Velvet da Vinci (San Francisco) and Contemporary Applied Arts (London). For Jo, "Using found objects is like starting the process of creating with part of the story already written. I choreograph, making introductions and interventions. The harmony of material, colour or repetition often compels the creation of groups or collections and each individual piece becomes a vehicle for the narrative, to enchant and communicate."

Joana Santos Porto, Portugal > p. 29
joanasantosjewellery@gmail.com | www.joanasantosjewellery.com
Joana's minimalist and geometric work is mostly inspired by architectural shapes, though also by nature and art. She contrasts the rationality of lines with delicate techniques and unpredictable detailing. The holder of a degree in architecture, Joana has achieved a genuine expression of her aesthetics in jewellery: straight angles and simple planes play with light and shadow, producing an exploration of three dimensionality and volumes. From the concept to the drawing and from the process to the matter, the jewellery pieces that she cultivates in her hands are pure.

Jorge Castañón Argentina > p. 114-115
info@jorgecastanon.com.ar | www.jorgecastanon.com.ar
"I talk about the broken and the damaged. About oblivion and the forgotten. About ourselves, and things of ours that are broken, and broken down. Things left under the rug, things that we've stabbed in the back, things that we can't face. I feel that I make fragile objects because we are fragile. My pieces grow old. And so do I. I talk about finitude."

José Luis Fettolini Barcelona, Spain / Residing in Bangkok, Thailand > p. 208
joseluis@workshopr2.com | www.fettolini.net
This jewellery designer and creative director has expansive professional experience of working with large fashion and jewellery firms. As an educator, he works with IED Barcelona and runs his own training platform, Workshop R2, which specializes in courses and master's degrees on design, brand creation and sustainability for the jewellery sector. He is involved in Fairmined certification, and he has advised mining communities and artisans on commercial entrepreneurship and development. He is the author of a book on sustainable jewellery that will soon be published through Promopress.

Joshua Kosker Takoma Park, MD, USA / Seneca, PA, USA > p. 196-197
joshuakosker@gmail.com | www.joshuakosker.com
Joshua is interested in how objects shape experiences and, in turn, how actions imprint meaning on the material world. Josh's research fuses traditional craft practices and unconventional processes – drawing from some of the most humble, discreet and commonly found materials – to explore universal and sometimes private subject matters in daily life. His work has been exhibited both nationally and internationally at various group exhibitions, and he has recently been included in several notable publications such as American Craft Magazine and Metalsmith Magazine. A recipient of the Ethical Metalsmiths Emerging Artist Award in 2014, Joshua earned his MFA in jewellery and metalsmithing from Bowling Green State University and his BFA from Indiana University of Pennsylvania.

Juhani Heikkilä Lahti, Finland / Residing in Helsinki, Finland > p. 132
hopeaheikkila@gmail.com | www. juhaniheikkila.fi
Juhani has been making jewellery art for over forty years. He has worked at the University of Industrial arts and Design in Helsinki, and he is now revisiting the passion of his youth: carving wood. His work starts with content and meanings. For example, his piece A Fishy Tale is a synonym for exaggeration and lies in all forms. For Juhani, artistic quality is highly important.

Julia Baudler Coburg, Germany / Residing in Berlin, Germany > p. 214
baudler.julia@gmail.com | www.julia-baudler.de
Julia studied both intermedia design and gemstone and jewellery design at the Hochschule Trier. Her work focuses on colours and also on various materials and forms. Colours are particularly important to Julia because of their ability to communicate different emotions. By contrast, the preciousness of the materials that she uses is not her top priority. What is much more important for her is that they have attractive colours and shapes and that they harmonize well with each other. By combining valuable materials with less valuable ones, she tries to create a tension in her pieces. However, most important of all for Julia is the fun and the pleasure involved in making her jewellery.

Julia deVille New Zealand / Residing in Melbourne, Australia > p. 44-45
julia@juliadeville.com | www.juliadeville.com
Julia deVille arrived in Australia from New Zealand on the cusp of adulthood and trained as a jeweller and taxidermist. Drawing on Renaissance, Baroque and Victorian aesthetics and ideas, she creates contemporary "memento mori" that arouse our curiosity through the use of paradoxical processes and materials. Her contemporary jewellery uses traditional precious and semiprecious metals, as well as gems, and occasionally materials that were once living, such as jet, human hair and taxidermy. Driven by a strong commitment to animal rights and an examination of mortality, Julia's work encourages viewers and wearers to identify with their own fate.

Julia Harrison Hopkinsville, KY, USA/Residing in Seattle, WA, USA > p. 34, 108-109
www.juliaharrison.net
As an artist specializing in small-scale carving, Julia spends much of her time "attacking small pieces of wood with even smaller pieces of metal," as she puts it. Her work has appeared in galleries and museums across the United States and in England, as well as in Exhibition in Print by Metalsmith Magazine. Julia also teaches workshops on wood and jewellery at venues such as the Penland School of Crafts, the Haystack Mountain School of Crafts, the 92nd St Y and Seattle's Pratt Fine Arts Center. Brooches exemplify what she loves about jewellery as a format: they allow art to go out into the world and connect with unpredictable audiences.

Julia Kraemer-Losereit Bielefeld, Germany / Residing inBraunschweig, Germany > p. 77
juli.k1@gmx.de | www.julia-kraemer-schmuck.de
Julia's work is based on the idea of lines in jewellery. In creating a line with thread, she produces various possibilities in terms of sequence, rhythm and structure. She is particularly interested in graphical lines and rhythmic ornamentation, and she finds excitement in discovering how multiple threads can form "open spaces for our thoughts and dreams." The main material used in her work is sewing thread. In addition, she works with lacquered aluminium and oxidized or enamelled silver, and sometimes she even uses hair and bones.

Julia Maria Künnap Tallinn, Estonia > p. 193
juliamaria@kynnap.ee | www. kynnap.ee
Julia Maria has taught at Alchimia, Florence, and at the Estonian Academy of Arts. She has reviewed MA and BA works at the Estonian Academy of Arts. Her works are held in public collections at the Estonian Applied Art Museum and the Art Hall, Tallinn, and in private collections in Estonia, Finland, Germany, Italy, Latvia and the United States. She has had solo exhibitions in Estonia, Italy and the United States. She uses natural stones that she grinds herself and precious metals.

Julia Obermaier Landau a. d. Isar, Germany / Residing in Kempten, Allgäu, Germany > p. 210
hello@juliaobermaier.com | www.juliaobermaier.com
Julia Obermaier lives and works in her own atelier in Kempten, Germany. She trained as a goldsmith at the State College for Glass and Jewellery in Kaufbeuren between 2009 and 2012. She then completed a BFA in gemstones and jewellery in Idar-Oberstein, Germany, in 2016. In creating delicate jewellery out of stone, Julia's main subject is personal spaces. Within her pieces, she creates rooms, containers, boxes or little caves, which are intended to be filled with one's own personal feelings, perceptions and sensations. Julia views her work as containers that protect the innermost emotions of the viewer or wearer and that can be used in the face of a hectic world.

>> K >>

Karen Vanmol Leuven, Belgium / Residing in Antwerp, Belgium > p. 138
karenvanmol@hotmail.com | www.karenvanmol.com
Karen Vanmol received a master's degree in 2010 from the Royal Academy of Fine Arts Antwerp. After graduating, she immediately started producing new work. To date, she has been selected for Schmuck 2015 and 2016 and Talente 20017, among other exhibitions. She has been a guest lecturer at Pxl-Mad Has-selt and RhOK-Academie in Brussels. "The inspiration for my work comes from close within myself. Cultivate is my view of human interaction with nature. That means nature becomes city life with a lot of restrictions and rules."

Karim Oukid Ouksel Ath Yani, Algeria / Residing in Barcelona, Spain > p. 70
arteyanibis@yahoo.es | www.karimoukid.com
Karim studied at the Berber Decorative Art School in Tizi Ouzou, Algeria. Since 2004, he has taught courses on Kabylian Berber jewellery at the Massana Art School in Barcelona, Spain. Furthermore, he has exhibited his work at the Ethnology Museum and at La Pedrera Museum in Barcelona, at the US Embassy in Algiers, and at the Folk Art Alliance Market in Santa Fe, USA. Karim employs silver, wood, enamels, Mediterranean coral and other stones in his pieces, which revive the memory and methods of ancient jewellers. More than decorative objects, they represent poems, histories, rivers, mountains, tastes, colours, flowers and his love for his homeland.

Karin Roy Andersson Umeå, Sweden / Residing in Gothenburg, Sweden > p. 18
karin@karin-roy.se | www.karin-roy.se
Repeated movements; multiplicity and recurrence are significant aspects of Karin's work. For Karin, variations between details are important. She creates structures and rhythms using small elements to build dynamic patterns. She has a strong interest in animals, especially fish and birds: "I love their shape, movements, the pattern of the feathers and scales – and their exceptional behaviour." Karin's pieces are made from recovered plastics. She looks for these materials everywhere – including in garbage containers and ditches – and is always on the hunt for that perfect material. Karin holds an MFA from Gothenburg's Academy of Design and Crafts, and since 2010 she has managed the jewellery gallery Four in the same city.

Karin Seufert Mannheim, Germany / Residing in Berlin, Germany > p. 117
kgseufert@gmx.de | www.karinseufert.de
Karin Seufert graduated from the Rietveld Academy in Amsterdam in 1995, where she studied under Professor Ruudt Peters. Since 1998, she has lived in Berlin, where she continues to develop her own work. She also lectures, conducts workshops, teaches and exhibits at home and abroad. PVC plays an important role in the realization of her concepts. All shapes in her pieces are made exclusively from small, punched circles of this material. The properties of the PVC as well as the patterns and structures that she applies create confusion as to the consistency of the jewellery. As Karin describes it, "Perception starts to fluctuate, heaviness turns into lightness, cold seems to be warm, while hardness softens."

Kate Dannenberg Philadelphia, PA, USA > p. 55
dannenbergjewelry@gmail.com | www.katedannenberg.com
Influenced by both the wilderness of upstate New York and urban experiences in the city of Philadelphia, Kate Dannenberg's work reflects an understanding of the nature of form, informed by a modern perspective. Kate studied metalsmithing and jewellery design at the School for American Crafts in Rochester, New York, and she has apprenticed with art jewellers. She is currently working as a bench jeweller and designer for a small, ethically minded, mission-driven jewellery company. Kate believes that as a result of her work and education, "I have developed a deep respect for handmade objects, the hands that make them, and the methods of making." Her method of working incorporates traditional techniques with a contemporary approach.

Katie Stormonth Brisbane, Australia > p. 123
info@katiestormonth.com | www.katiestormonth.com
Katie Stormonth is a contemporary jeweller based in Brisbane, Australia. She is one of the founding members of Bench, a collective jewellery studio. She completed a BFA in 2011 and currently works as the technical officer at Queensland College of Art, Griffith University. As an emerging artist, she participates regularly in exhibitions both in Brisbane and across Australia. Her practice aims to expand the boundaries of wearable body adornment through experimentation with materials and forms. She constructs alluring arrangements of repetitious forms and painted surfaces, highlighting the patterns of bold and decorative chased line work and aiming to provoke the wearer to both see and feel the pieces.

Katja Prins Haarlem, The Netherlands / Residing in Amsterdam, The Netherlands > p. 184
info@katjaprins.com | www.katjaprins.com
Katja Prins graduated from the Gerrit Rietveld Academy in 1997 and has been working as an independent jewellery artist ever since. Her work has been exhibited in galleries and museums all over Europe, Asia, the United States and Canada, and it is represented in a variety of museum collections. In addition to exhibiting, she also lectures and teaches internationally.

Kim Eric Lilot San Francisco, CA, USA > p. 55
kimlilot@sbcglobal.net | www.KimEricLilot.com
Kim's relationship with his art is a deeply personal one: "As an artist I have learned to live with the knowledge of the precious and ephemeral nature of beauty and life. It is the concurrent awareness of my own mortality that impels me to live in the immediate moment and that, in turn, inspires me to work towards transforming this personal sense of wonder, awe and primal fear into creative expression."

Kye-Yeon Son South Korea / Residing in Canada > p. 28
kson@nscad.ca
A winner of the 2011 Saidye Bronfman Award – one of Canada's prestigious Governor General's Awards in Visual and Media Arts – Kye-Yeon Son earned a BFA in applied art in 1979 at Seoul National University and an MFA in 1984 at Indiana University. Son joined the faculty of NSCAD University, Canada, in 1995. Inspired by the persistent transformation of bare tree trunks and branches during winter, he interprets their emotive qualities such as resilience, endurance and fragility by abstracting essence from forms. Employing the inherent physical characteristics of fine metal wire allows him to portray a variety of expressive qualities in the branches through lines, structure, volume, space, colour, light and shadow.

>> L >>

Lee Heejin Daegu, South Korea > p. 39
jina011105@gmail.com
Lee Heejin expresses the uniqueness of the figurative characteristics of wildflowers through jewellery. Wildflowers have bright and soft natural colours, and in order to express them and their harmonious relationship with nature, most of Lee Heejin's works use silver as a material and bring out its distinctive colour.

Lena Wunderlich Ostercappeln, Germany / Residing in Berlin, Germany > p. 101
lwunderl@alumni.risd.edu | www.lenawunderlich.de
Lena Wunderlich is an artist based in Berlin, Germany. She graduated with a fine arts degree from Rhode Island School of Design. Although Lena's work is subtle or minimal in appearance, it beguilingly reveals complexities regarding the body. The sensations of touch, texture and tension are relayed through her creations, which expand our understanding of jewellery.

Leticia Llera Mexico City, Mexico > p. 90
letyllera@gmail.com | www.leticiallera.com
For more than twenty-four years, Leticia Llera has been creating countless pieces by mixing two of her greatest passions: jewellery and her homeland. She studied jewellery metalsmithing techniques at the National Fine Arts Institute, where she found in metals the perfect way to express herself and to transform creativity into something tangible, leaving part of herself in every detail. Leticia has been involved in various exhibitions, courses, workshops and national and international awards. Her most recent accolades include her selection for Savor Silver/The Silver Institute: International Jewellery Designers because of her original and precise silver creations.

Liaung-Chung Yen Taichung, Taiwan / Residing in Henrietta, NY, USA > p. 134, 188
liaung@yahoo.com | www.liaungchungyen.com
Liaung-Chung Yen's jewellery and artistic aesthetic are influenced by Chinese culture and art. Yen sees his work as an expression of the mind, and also as small sculptures that document the time in which he lives and its emotions. His inspiration comes from the structures of nature, landscape and architecture. The materials that he uses are mostly 18k gold, sterling silver and precious stones. He is the recipient of numerous awards, including an MJSA Vision Award, a New York Foundation for the Arts Fellowship and a NICHE Award. His work has been exhibited at several prestigious shows such as the Philadelphia Museum of Art Contemporary Craft Show, the Smithsonian Craft Show and Sculpture Objects Functional Art and Design, Chicago.

Lin Cheung Basingstoke, Hampshire, UK > p. 201
www.lincheung.co.uk
Lin Cheung is a jewellery artist, designer and senior lecturer at Central Saint Martins. She trained at the Royal College of Art and lives and works in the UK. Her approach to designing and making questions the established and authorised uses and meanings of jewellery and objects. Her work is a personal response to everyday experiences and observations. Lin works independently and collaboratively on private and public commissions, personal research projects and design projects. She has won several awards for her work and exhibits internationally in major museums and galleries.

Lital Mendel Israel > p. 29
mendelital@gmail.com | litalmendel.com
Lital Mendel graduated with a degree in jewellery design from the Shenkar College of Engineering and Design in Israel, and she is a member of the jewellery collective fKlimt02. After producing a few collections dealing with repetitive patterns, order and structure and making some very delicate pieces, Lital began to feel disillusioned: "I felt like destroying, burning, tearing jewellery apart," she says. And so she developed a new way of creating jewellery, through which she tries to preserve the exact dividing line between designed and deformed. This new approach has clear links to her previous collections, but it is less inhibited and more unplanned – "and maybe even reckless," she observes. The process involves taking jewellery made for previous collections and then applying all sorts of material manipulations to the pieces, which allows her to preserve some part of the old object while simultaneously disfiguring other parts.

Lluís Comín Barcelona, Spain > p. 160
info@lluiscomin.com
Lluís was born in Barcelona in 1958, and he studied jewellery at the Escola Massana, graduating in 1981. He is recognized as a gemmologist and diamond specialist by the University of Barcelona and the Gemmological Association of Great Britain, but he learned to be a jeweller in the workshop with his father. He has a space that is open to the public where people can see his work, and in addition to having done exhibitions in several countries in Europe and the Americas, his works can be seen in private collections and museums. He sees jewellery as a means of artistic communication and not simply as a form of ornamentation, and he believes that the relationship between a piece and its wearer is a unique and enriching experience for both parties.

Lou Sautreau France / Residing in Belgium > p. 24
lou.sautreau@gmail.com | lousautreau.com
After studying textile design in France and in England, Lou Sautreau decided to move to Belgium to master fine and contemporary jewellery. For the past two years, Lou has attempted to arouse jewellery wearers' curiosity and disturb their perceptions of the familiar aspects of their environment. Lou likes to mix poor materials with precious ones and textile techniques with jewellery ones. The underlying idea is to play with these contrasts and to give an unexpected shape to these materials through producing geometric, unique and playful bracelets, rings, brooches and earrings.

Luci Jockel Indiana, PA, USA > p. 40, 102
lucirjockel@gmail.com | www.lucijockel.com
Luci Jockel holds an MFA in jewellery and metalsmithing (2016) from Rhode Island School of Design and a BFA from Indiana University of Pennsylvania (2014). Her work has been shown at various venues, including Galerie Marzee's International Graduate Show 2016, where she received the Marzee International Graduate Prize; East Carolina University's Metal Symposium (2016); and the Society of North American Goldsmiths' Juried Student Exhibition (2015). Her work has been featured in American Craft Magazine, Klimt02, Beautiful Bizarre and other publications. Her work explores the lost relationship between human and nonhuman through wearable art by connecting animal bones, insect specimens and dried flora to the body with metal.

Lucie Houdková Brno, Czech Republic / Residing in Prague, Czech Republic > p. 32-33
lucie.houdkova@centrum.cz | www.luciehoudkova.com
A graduate of the Academy of Arts, Architecture and Design in Prague, Lucie Houdková began her studies in the metal and jewellery atelier of the sculptor V. K. Novák and completed them in the atelier of Eva Eisler. She uses both non-traditional and traditional materials in her work. She sees designing new jewellery as a process that involves experimentation and playing with material. In recent years, her inspiration has come in particular from natural organic forms. Lucie endeavours to achieve a certain kind of harmony and balance through her work. In her view, a jewellery piece completes the personality of its wearer, but at the same time it is a work of art in itself.

Lucie Majerus Luxembourg > p. 189
majeruslucie@gmail.com | www.majeruslucie.eu
Lucie Majerus is a recent graduate of the Design Academy Eindhoven. As a designer, she likes to question and make people question the ordinary, to trigger their imagination and playfulness, and to make them smile for a moment. She turns to the past to understand how things are today so that she can imagine the future. Her interests lie in conceptual thinking, social cohesion and material experiments, as well as in senses, experiences and memories. She takes a multidisciplinary approach that encompasses food, textiles, colours and illustration as well as jewellery.

>> M >>

Magali Thibault Quebec, Canada / Residing in St-Lambert, Quebec, Canada > p. 198-199
info@magalithibaultgobeil.com | www.magalithibaultgobeil.com
Driven by the desire to contribute to the field of contemporary jewellery, but also to transform and change it, Magali Thibault's work is based on exploring emotions through form and colour. Although she was trained by her artist parents and was also partly self-taught, she graduated from the Jewellery School of Montreal in 2013. Throughout her young career, her innovative work has been recognized through several prizes, awards and distinctions. In 2014, she was a finalist in the renowned François-Houdé competition, and she received the first presence prize at the Salon des métiers d'art de Montréal. In 2013, she was a finalist at the Niche Awards in Philadelphia. The L. A. Pai Gallery in Ottawa and the Galerie Noel Guyomarc'h in Montreal now present her work.

Mallory Weston United States / Residing in Philadelphia, PA, USA > p. 110
malloryweston@gmail.com | www.malloryweston.com
Mallory Weston's work involves a marriage between traditional jewellery techniques and textile techniques, and she creates large-scale wearable pieces that allow metal to move with the fluidity of fabric. Mallory received her MFA in jewellery and metalsmithing from Rhode Island School of Design in 2013. She currently works as a professor of jewellery at several Philadelphia-area colleges and universities. She maintains an active studio practice as a member of the JV Collective, a group of five female art jewellers. Her work was recently featured in a solo exhibition at Sienna Patti Contemporary entitled Of Ophidia. Her work can be found in the permanent collection of the CODA Museum and in the Stedelijk Museum 's-Hertogenbosch in the Netherlands.

Mareen Alburg Hennigsdorf, Germany / Residing in Halle, Germany > p. 167
mail@mareenalburg.de | www.mareenalburg.de
I studied jewellery at Burg Giebichenstein, University of Art and Design in Halle, where I live and work. I like to create brooches that She creates brooches that play with form, volume and weight. The interior and exterior elements of my pieces interact with one another to open up the mind of the observer.

Maria Diez Serrat Barcelona > p. 187

info@mariadiezserrat.com | www.mariadiezserrat.com

Maria Diez Serrat's creative process is based on her everyday environment. Once she starts to examine an image, an object or a detail, her initial impulse leads her to play with it by photographing, manipulating, blurring or reproducing it, or by adding elements or colour. The process produces a design when it manages to surprise her, something that comes about when the object or image in her hands takes on a life of its own. What was once an inanimate thing becomes something with feeling – and therefore something that makes her feel. Maria is drawn to the fact that this moment can be turned into a piece of jewellery that someone will wear.

Maria Rosa Franzin Tripoli, Libya / Residing in Padua, Italy > p. 71

mariarosafranzin11@gmail.com

I am a teacher at the Liceo Artistico Pietro Selvatico in Padua. I look for distinctive signs in my own work by observing the response of metal to heat from the fire. I started thinking about these pieces as small containers and as volumes described by a kind of "incorrect" geometry: constructions that are free in their form rather than defined by symmetry. In some of these pieces I added a wall of resin, or a bosso wood, with a rough surface to divide the space. I regard these little places as "case dell' anima" (houses of the soul), culminations of vital actions and past passions that are hidden but not forgotten.

Marion Blume Munich, Germany / Residing in Amsterdam, The Netherlands > p. 107

mail@marionblume.com | www.marionblume.com

My jewellery journey began in 2007 when I started a goldsmithing apprenticeship at the School for Goldsmithing in Pforzheim, Germany. After gaining the technical knowledge required to produce jewellery, I developed my artistic language at the Rietveld Academy in Amsterdam. The first project that I undertook after I graduated in 2016 was called Branch – No Branch, a series dedicated to human perception. At first glance, the brooches in the series look like branches without bark. But to sharp-eyed observers who don't take things for granted, a different reality is revealed: the small, branch-like sculptures are manmade pieces that are carved out of a block made up of many thin layers of wood.

Marta Roca Barcelona / Residing in Tarragona > p. 135

martaroca.sole@gmail.com | martarocacontemporaryjewelry.blogspot.com.es

Barcelona-born Marta Roca started out in the world of jewellery in 2008 and graduated in 2012 from an artistic jewellery programme at the Escola Massana in Barcelona. From her studio in a small village in the Tarragona region of Catalonia, she has worked alongside artistic jewellers such as Enric Majoral and Grego García Tebar from Galeria Amaranto Joies. She is interested in jewellery as a means of transforming material, as artistic expression, and as a way of life. Her passion for objects and for observing them is what moves her to produce new creations. She focuses on their details, colours and forms, and she attempts to make them communicate a new language when they are worn on the body. "When I work with my materials, I realise that they will tell me what the next step is," she says.

Melissa Cameron Perth, Australia / Residing in Seattle, WA > p. 97

jewellery@melissacameron.net | melissacameron.net

Australian-born artist Melissa Cameron lives and works in Seattle. She received an MFA in jewellery and metalsmithing from Monash University and a BA in interior architecture from Curtin University in Australia. Her works can be found, among other places, in the collections of the National Gallery of Australia, the Cheongju City Collection in South Korea and the Arts Centre Melbourne. Melissa's jewellery works are the result of her ongoing research into architecture, geometry, social justice and the human body. Through her works, she aims to reinforce our understanding of the interdependence of all matter, and the sacredness of every human life.

Monika Brugger Wehr, Germany / Residing in Héde-Bazouges, France > p. 42, 175

monkbrugge@gmail.com | monikabrugger.eu

Monika Brugger develops her jewellery pieces as though she was carrying out an etymological investigation. The central feature of her work is not a particular connection between form and substance, but rather the idea, the category and the tradition of language. Her art is in a certain sense conceptual, and it involves an interrogation of the relationship between the agreed word and the thing made. Her works are often made using highly traditional techniques that have been regarded as crafts and "feminine" practices – for example, embroidery or sewing. In Monika's view, jewellery is perceived as a social indicator as much as it is a handmade object based on technical and aesthetic choices. She also sees pieces as sentimental objects and objects of memory, often inherited through matrilineal filiations.

Montserrat Lacomba Girona, Catalonia, Spain > p. 212

montlacomba@gmail.com | www.montserratlacomba.com

Montserrat Lacomba holds a BFA from the University of Barcelona, and she has taught jewellery courses at Barcelona's Massana School. In 2000, she started to create jewellery. She likes to experiment, and she has worked with different materials such as silver, copper, enamels, fabric and resin. In 2008, she began a blog called Mar de Color Rosa, through which she compiles and shares information about contemporary jewellery. From 2009 until 2013, she was a member of Joyas Sensacionales, a group coordinated by jeweller Silvia Walz in Barcelona. In 2014, she opened her workshop in Girona to the public in order to present both her own work and exhibitions of contemporary jewellery by other artists.

>> N >>

Natalie Hoogeveen Huizen, The Netherlands > p. 116

Info@nataliehoogeveen.nl | www.nataliehoogeveen.nl

Natalie completed her training as a goldsmith in Amsterdam in 2004. She then studied jewellery design in Schoonhoven in the Netherlands. The jewellery pieces that Natalie makes are inspired by exciting personal stories, which she translates into unique, handmade works that are aesthetic, playful, vivacious and colourful and often feature a humorous twist. Natalie works with silver and gold, and she loves to incorporate different kinds of materials like precious stones, enamel, found objects and natural products. The series that she has made include Dutch Sayings, Madagascar and Memories.

Nico Sales Madrid, Spain / Residing in Palma de Mallorca, Spain > p. 149

nicosales.1990@gmail.com

Until he decided to start a new life by moving to Mallorca to study jewellery and work in the Darmunt studio in Palma, Nico Sales had always lived in the world of the theatre. At present, he is studying artistic jewellery at ESADIB. During these years of his training, he has studied, considered and defined his style, his way of thinking and the foundations of his work. "I create pieces for human beings," Nico says. "I use my body as a blank page on which I make my designs and as a stepping stone in bringing them to completion. My jewellery recounts my story and my failures up until this moment in my life."

Nicole Taubinger Munich, Germany / Residing in Prague, Czech Republic > p. 110

ntaubing14@gmail.com | NicoleTaubingerART/Facebook

"I studied metalsmithing and jewellery at the University of Oregon in Eugene. To create my pieces, I use nearly new objects made from polymers, which I believe are so ubiquitous that we scarcely notice them. I collect these items from the street, containers or scrapyards and place them in a new context to make them visible again and to express the multifaceted nature of society and its paradoxes, which I perceive as our "second nature". Whereas indigenous people htorically used seeds and pits to create their jewellery, the polymers that I use in my pieces are the seeds and pits of that second nature."

>> O >>

Odd Studio Athens, Greece > p. 80-81

oddstudio7@gmail.com | www.odd-studio.net

Odd Studio is an art collective that designs and creates handmade jewellery. It is triggered creatively when it sets itself a challenge by selecting a field for investigation and then using the team's diversity as a tool to research, analyse, design and craft in order to produce jewellery as the end result.

>> P >>

Pallavi Verma Lucknow, Uttar Pradesh, India / Residing in Mumbai, Maharashtra, India > p. 161

pallavivermadesigns@gmail.com

Pallavi is an Indian contemporary jewellery designer who completed her bachelor's and master's degrees at the Royal Academy of Fine Arts in Antwerp, Belgium. Her MA project, entitled Intimation (2016), incorporates personal experiences from both Eastern and Western culture. This family-focused project is about femininity and hidden revelations, as well as about marking boundaries, emotions and identity. Pallavi makes interactive pieces through which she tries to involve/touch the wearer and the viewer physically and introspectively She currently works in the area of research and innovation at the Indian Institute of Gems and Jewellery in Mumbai.

Pamela de la Fuente Santiago de Chile > p. 120
pamela@pameladelafuente.cl | www.pameladelafuente.cl
An artist and art historian at the University of Chile who has completed specialist studies in Mexico, Argentina, Spain, Germany and Italy, Pamela has been teaching jewellery since 2003. She set up a school that bears her name, and she was the founder of JoyaBrava, the first association of Chilean contemporary jewellers. Her work focuses on teaching and management, through which she contributes to the development of jewellery in Chile today. Highlights of her work as a jewellery maker include her creation of innovative series. At the start of the new millennium, she became involved in creating jewellery from recycled computer components, thereby giving life to objects, forms and materials that were not destined to become jewellery.

Patrícia Domingues Lisbon/Residing in Idar-Oberstein. Germany > p. 128
info@patriciadomingues.pt | www.patriciadomingues.pt
Patrícia's studies have taken her beyond her native Portugal to Spain, Estonia and, most recently, Idar-Oberstein in Germany, where she completed her master's degree in art jewellery and now resides. Her work has been recognized through awards such as New Traditional Jewellery (2012), Talente (2014) and the Mary Funaky Award (2014). Patricia is currently a PhD student in arts at the University of Hasselt and PXL–MAD in Belgium. "I have been interested in the idea of recreating an image of a landscape through processes of fragmentation, working with 'the line' as a medium for construction and separation. Blocks of material are consciously fragmented in a rationalized breaking, which simultaneously frees and demarcates a form from a space, and are later reunited."

Patricia López Piedrahita Bogotá, Colombia > p. 76
murundwaproyectoornamento@gmail.com
"I am a visual artist by profession, an artisan by vocation, and a jewellery maker by devotion," declares Patricia López Piedrahita. She has spent twenty-five years learning and developing her vision of the craft. Her Inicio collection hints at evocative ideas such as arriving home and recalling life experiences, as well as at questions of love and the heart."

Paul Adie Glasgow, Scotland / Residing in Munich, Germany > p. 162
hello@pauladie.com | www.pauladie.com
After studying Spanish and Russian philology in his native Scotland, and after a few years working as a translator in Barcelona, Paul Adie decided to dedicate his life to what had always fascinated him: artistic jewellery. He began his artistic education at the Escola Massana, Barcelona, and he is currently continuing his postgraduate studies at the Academy of Fine Arts, Munich. In the 2015/2016 academic year, he was an artist in residence at the Glasgow School of Art, and he has participated in important competitions such as Talente 2016 and the 2016 Mari Funaki Contemporary Jewellery Award.

Paul McClure Toronto, Ontario, Canada > p. 147
pmcclure@sympatico.ca | www.paulmcclure.com
Paul McClure's jewellery is held in various museum collections, including those of the Montreal Museum of Fine Arts, the Design Museum of Barcelona and National Museums Scotland. He studied at NSCAD University, Canada (BFA, 1989); Escola Massana, Spain; and NCAD, Ireland (MA, 1999). In 2015, Paul received the Saidye Bronfman Prize, a Governor General of Canada Award – the highest distinction given to Canadian visual artists. He is a professor in the jewellery department of Toronto's George Brown College. Ornamentation and jewellery's relationship to the body are central themes in Paul's sculptural pieces. The scientific fields of biology, pathology and genetics inspire his work, as does anatomical, microscopic and digital imaging of the human body. His jewellery reflects our increasingly digital and biotechnological understanding of mortality.

Paula Estrada Medellín, Colombia > p. 48
estradapaula@hotmail.com | www.paulaestradamatyasova.com
Paula is an industrial designer whose background is in furniture and fashion companies. She discovered the jewellery world after seeking out a space in which she could create, imagine and communicate as she pleased, unencumbered by the rules and requirements of the industrial and commercial sectors. For Paula, jewellery is not just about decorating the body. It is also an act of communication that contains memory and links the soul with the world. She sees jewellery as the perfect three-dimensional field because it is multidisciplinary and fuses multiple worlds and visions. "It is about the construction of objects, aesthetics, design methods, and the intimate act of communicating," she says. "Objects can be like jewellery pieces, jewellery can be like objects, and both have souls of their own."

Paula Zuker Buenos Aires, Argentina / Residing in Chile > p. 73
pzuker@hotmail.com | paulazuker.blogspot.cl
Contemporary jewellery workshops are something that I have become hooked on as part of my er-ratic and spontaneous training," says Paula Zuker. This Argentine designer has been involved in group exhibitions in Argentina, Chile and Italy. In 2016, she received the Argentina Jewellery Prize at the first Buenos Aires Contemporary Jewellery Biennial. Paula was a photographer before she became a jewellery maker, but as she comments, "You never stop being anything." And so it is that she takes her inspiration from the layers and depths of photography, and from the simultaneous stories that it tells. She focuses on daily life, loved ones, ordinary moments and functional objects: "Discovering new scenes and stories in these happens almost inevitably", she says.

Piero Acuto – AQTO Turin, Italy > p. 129
aqtomailbox@gmail.com | it-it.facebook.com/aqtotorino
Behind the brand AQTO lurks the eclectic figure of Piero Acuto, a musician, composer and graphic designer. He might be described, citing Brian Eno, as an "oblique strategist of expression. Piero is an artist who succeeds in his almost subliminal use of worlds and single elements that are only in appearance unmatchable. Piero uses pliers, coping saws, steel files, small drills and sometimes specialist tools of his own invention. His handicraft techniques bring about a metamorphosis of materials that produces unique jewellery.

Pornruedee Boonyapan Bangkok, Thailand > p. 204
pornruedeeboonyapan@gmail.com | www.cherryboonyapan.com
Pornrudee (Cherry) Boonyapan's educational background is in fine and applied arts. In 2007, she studied jewellery design and devices at the School for Goldsmiths and Watchmakers in Pforzheim, Germany. After graduating as a jewellery designer, she participated in several group exhibitions around Europe. She was chosen as a jewellery designer in residence by Spreeglanz Berlin. In 2015, she completed an MFA in Idar-Oberstein, Germany. She is now an artistic jeweller and designer who works as the manager of Atta Gallery in Bangkok.

>> R >>

Ralph Bakker Kürten, Germany / Residing in Rotterdam, The Netherlands > p. 82
ralph@luna.nl | www.ralphbakker.nl
Ralph Bakker lives and works in Rotterdam. He has been a jewellery maker since 1993. The galleries that he has worked with include Rob Koudijs in the Netherlands, Antonella Villanova in Italy, Slavik in Austria and Tactile in Switzerland. He has participated in numerous group exhibitions, and his works are held in several private and public collections.

Ramón Puig Cuyàs Mataró, Catalonia, Spain / Residing in Vilanova i la Geltrú, Catalonia, Spain > p. 194-195
puigcuyas@gmail.com | puigcuyas2.blogspot.com.es
Ramón Puig Cuyàs graduated from Barcelona's Escola Massana in 1974 and has been a member of its faculty since 1977, teaching courses on design and jewellery making. He is a prominent, internationally renowned art jeweller and has served as a visiting professor at a wide number of schools and universities in Canada, Denmark, Estonia, Finland, France, Italy, Germany, Portugal, the Netherlands and the UK. Since 1974, Ramón's work has been featured in hundreds of galleries and museums across the world. His pieces can be found in the most important public and private jewellery collections in Europe, the United States and Canada.

Rita Soto Chile > p. 26
rita.soto@gmail.com | www.ritasoto.cl
In her work as a jewellery maker, Rita Soto constantly explores and develops her identity in terms of its language and materiality. As part of this search, she discovered the traditional horsehair fabric made in central Chile. Her pieces are the result of her efforts to bring new meaning to horsehair. She has taken what she has learned and altered proportions and dimensions, exploring the strength and fragility of the raw material and the limits of its forms. They reinterpret a tradition that is timeless and limitless, and they make and unmake the fabric, suggesting the passage of time between one's fingers.

Robert Thomas Mullen Freeburg, IL, USA / Residing in St. Louis, MO, USA > p. 201
robertthomasmullen@gmail.com | www.robertthomasmullen.com
Robert Thomas Mullen maintains a studio in St. Louis, where he also teaches at Craft Alliance. His work is represented by the Houston Center for Contemporary Craft, Penland Gallery, the Society for Contemporary Craft and Craft Alliance. He holds an MFA in metalsmithing from the Edinboro University of Pennsylvania. His pieces have been exhibited nationally and internationally. Memory is a key theme in Robert's recent projects: "Over the years, my memories slowly deteriorate and play tricks on me. I have trouble remembering things that were once quite clear to me," he says. "In my newest work, I juxtapose the real with the fabricated freely, just as my recollections deceive me."

Robyn Wilson Melbourne, Australia > p. 134
robyn@robynwilsonjeweller.com | www.robynwilsonjeweller.com
For Robyn Wilson, the hand making of objects has always been a deeply rewarding practice. Inspired by strong colours and bold shapes, Robyn uses materials such as Argentium silver and Monel, and she lends an added dimension to her pieces through hydraulic pressing. After a long career as an IT specialist, Robyn's path to contemporary jewellery was fuelled by discovering a passion for working with Argentium silver. She then completed an advanced diploma in engineering technology and jewellery at Melbourne Polytechnic. She was awarded the Design Institute of Australia's Victorian Graduate of the Year for Jewellery in 2014.

Rodrigo Acosta Arias Mendoza, Argentina / Residing in Valencia, Spain > p. 49
rodrigoacostacrea@gmail.com | www.acostarodrigo.com | www.viruthiers.com
My work is based on investigating the connection that can be established between jewellery and the diversity of garments, as well as on exploring jewellery's relationship with memory and the body. I am interested in the relationships that people develop with their bodies through the garments they wear and show or conceal. I consider garments and the memory and traces – both physical and mental – that they leave on the wearer to be part of a process of deconstruction and rebuilding. My search for the new often leads me toward disorder and chaos, because, I need to be carried away by what I feel and experience, by the natural or inner impulse that provokes an action or a feeling, free of prejudice, without awareness of reason."

Rosa Nogués Reus, Catalonia, Spain / Residing in Barcelona, Catalonia, Spain > p. 148
rosanoguesfreixas@gmail.com | rosanogues.com
Rosa Nogués was born in Reus in 1983. She studied jewellery at the Escola Massana and pharmacy at the University of Barcelona. Her pieces have been exhibited in Barcelona and all over Europe, as well as in China and Colombia. She was a recipient of the Young Talent Prize awarded by Belgium's WCC-BF Gallery. Rosa explores the timeless themes of life and the irrevocable passing of time. Her pieces invite us to capture life moments in the inexorable passing of the seasons and convey a lively sense of immortality. Metamorphosis and adaptation are the main ideas in her work.

>> S >>

Samuel Guillén Caracas, Venezuela / Residing in New York, NY, USA > p. 181
guillensamuel@gmail.com | www.samuelguillen.com
Venezuelan jewellery maker and designer Samuel Guillén trained under the mentorship of Susan Sloan and Klaus Bürgel in New York. Samuel's main inspiration is the everyday experience of the urban landscape. His creative approach is driven by systematically investigating how to transform urban complexity, which is often made of rough, straightforward technical elements, into a visual source for jewellery. To that end, he systematically photographs fragments of the city that he might consider inspiring; this photographic research always constitutes the start of his creative process. Samuel's pieces are all unique, and they are usually made from silver using hollow construction techniques. His work has been exhibited in Venezuela, Brazil and New York.

Selen Ozus Istanbul, Turkey > p. 220
selenozus@gmail.com | www.selenozus.com
Selen Özus received her BFA in ceramic and glass design from Mimar Sinan Fine Art University, and she completed a three-year jewellery programme at Alchimia Contemporary Jewellery School, Florence. She currently lives in Istanbul and works as an instructor at Maden Contemporary Jewellery Studio, which she founded with her colleague Burcu Büyükünal. According to Selen, "The sensations created by everybody and everything awaken a desire to produce" in her, and her creative process "all starts with the valuable beauties and ugliness that surround us: people, being human, lights, spaces, relations, memories, nature and details."

Sharareh Aghaei Tehran, Iran / Residing in Idar-Oberstein, Germany > p. 139
sharareh.aghaei@yahoo.com
After starting my artistic education with a BA in arts and handicrafts at the University of Tehran, I worked for four years as a freelancer. In 2013, I continued my development as a designer at the Idar-Oberstein campus of the Hochschule Trier, where I studied gemstone and jewellery design, graduating with a BFA in 2014 and an MFA in 2017. These degrees also provided me with the opportunity to complete an exchange semester at the Alchimia contemporary jewellery school in Florence. My key source of inspiration is the notion of identity, the different layers and networks of which I express through weaving techniques.

Sharon Massey Winston-Salem, NC / Residing in Pittsburgh, PA > p. 119
sharon@sharon-massey.com | www.sharon-massey.com
Sharon Massey is a professor of jewellery and metals at Indiana University of Pennsylvania. Her jewellery is inspired by the postindustrial landscape of Pittsburgh and the surrounding areas. Although this region has shifted from a reliance on coal, steel and manufacturing, remnants of that past remain. Smokestacks, chimneys and other masonry edifices are scattered like monuments around the region, dominating both the urban landscape and the surrounding countryside. Sharon's Brickwork series of jewellery uses copper and enamel to imitate masonry structures and abstract familiar architectural forms.

Sigurd Bronger Oslo, Norway > p. 211
sbronge@online.no
Sigurd Bronger is known for his mechanical constructions filled with humour and surprising elements. His art pieces are transportation devices for everyday objects such as a shoe soles, sponges or eggs. His work has been acquired by important museums such as the V&A in London, Het Stedelijk Museum in Amsterdam and the Nationalmuseum in Stockholm. In 2012, he received the Torsten and Wanja Söderberg Prize. The prize committee commented that Sigurd's works "invite us on a journey into a mechanical wonderland, full of boys' dreams and romantic, joyful pranks. Sigurd Bronger takes us back to the early design language of industrialism and the innovations of the Renaissance, or forward to utopian visions of the future."

Silvia Walz Germany / Residing in Vilanova i la Geltrú, Catalonia, Spain > p. 209
silviawalz@gmail.com | www.silviawalz.com
Silvia Walz studied at the Fachhochschule Hildesheim and at Barcelona's Escola Massana. She lives and works Vilanova i la Geltrú, near Barcelona. She teaches at the Escola Massana, and since 2008 she has also taught at the Taller Perill, which she founded. Her works have been selected for individual and group exhibitions in various European countries, as well as in Russia, China, the United States and Canada.

Sim Luttin Melbourne, Australia > p. 145, 159
simluttin@gmail.com | www.simluttin.com
After completing a BFA at RMIT University in Melbourne, Sim Luttin undertook an associateship at JamFactory: Contemporary Craft and Design in Adelaide and an MFA in metalsmithing and jewellery design at Indiana University in Bloomington. Her major achievements include receiving Australia Council for the Arts emerging and mid-career research grants to develop new work. These awards have resulted in solo exhibitions in Adelaide, Melbourne, Sydney and Bloomington. She has also participated in numerous prestigious group shows. Her current work plots courses across time and examines notions of memory, ritual, personal authenticity and materiality. Her work features in the collections of the Marzee Gallery and the Art Gallery of South Australia, as well as in notable private collections worldwide. She has also been featured in several Lark Books and Promopress publications.

Snem Yildirim Ankara, Turkey / Residing in Istanbul, Turkey > p. 62-63
yildirimsnem@gmail.com | studio-zigzag.com | www.snemyildirim.com
After graduating from Gazi University's department of architecture, in 2011 Snem Yildirim began a master's in architectural design at Istanbul Bilgi University. She then worked as an architect but subsequently turned toward jewellery by taking a leather footwear and accessories design course at Istanbul Moda Academy. She then fulfilled a long-held dream by setting up Studio Zigzag, a contemporary jewellery firm. Snem creates by taking inspiration from the cultural texture and the surroundings of the world around her, which provide the diversity and contrasts that produce the colours of her works. Through her materials and production techniques, she blends contrasts between East and West, the local and the global, the traditional and the modern, and the geometric and the organic.

Sol Flores Argentina> p. 14-15

solfloresjoyeria@gmail.com

At the age of eleven, I began to attend La Nave, the studio of the great Jorge Castañón. Since then, I have been involved in various national and international exhibitions, beginning in 1999 at the Centro Cultural San Martin in Buenos Aires and going as far afield as Schmuck 2015 in Munich. Contemporary jewellery offers escapism and expression. In my collections, I aim to create by using discarded materials destined for the garbage pile and oblivion, as well as the most ridiculous objects possible. I put these components together in awkward and incoherent combinations. Learning to fly is not easy, and neither is learning to fall. But living with your feet on the ground – that's boring!

Sondra Sherman Philadelphia, PA / Residing in San Diego, CA > p. 185

ssherman@sdsu.edu | www.sondra-sherman.com

Sondra Sherman's work explores the distinctive voice of jewellery and the psychological and social context of the body and wearer. She is programme head of jewellery and metalwork at San Diego State University. Sondra received a diploma degree from the Academy of Fine Arts in Munich, Germany, where she resided for ten years. Sondra's awards include individual artist fellowships from the Rhode Island Council on the Arts, the Louis Comfort Tiffany Foundation Emerging Artists Fellowship, an artist fellowship from Pennsylvania Council on the Arts, a Mid-Atlantic Regional National Endowment for the Arts and a Fulbright Scholarship for Study Abroad.

Stephen Bottomley Norwich, England, UK / Residing in Birmingham, UK > p. 86

stephenbottomley@hotmail.com | klimt02.net/jewellers/stephen-bottomley

Professor Stephen Bottomley is head of the school of jewellery at Birmingham City University. He trained at the Royal College of Art (1999–2001). He was previously head of department of Jewellery and silversmithing at Edinburgh College of Art, Scotland (2008-2017) and chairman of the UK Association for Contemporary Jewellery (2005-2007). Inspired by the rhythm and patterns found in oriental motifs and mathematical geometry, his work seeks to capture their inherent beauty in fine metalwork and contemporary jewellery. He combines digital technologies and the ancient goldsmith's craft to translate these surfaces' qualities to metal via etching and printing techniques. Vitreous enamel is often applied to his jewellery to reinforce the animated state of these enriched patterns through transparent coloured layers.

Susanne Matsché Anderson, SC, USA / Residing in Berlin, Germany > p. 20

mail@susannematsche.com | www.susannematsche.com

Susanne studied at the Vienna Academy of Applied Arts. She was a guest student at the jewellery department of the Stroganoff Institute of Applied Arts in Moscow and at FH Pforzheim, Germany. She has exhibited her work in Europe, the United States and Japan. Susanne has a somewhat complex relationship with jewellery. I love the delicate and intimate detail of jewellery, but sometimes it seems so unnecessary and a useless luxury. Yet it is this luxury that makes it all worthwhile. No one needs this message and no one asks for this downer to be put on their chest, but I feel the need to make these precious pieces come to life. This contradiction between the message in the brooch and the precious tradition of filigree and traditional techniques is what entices me.

>> T >>

Tala Yuan Jieyang, Guandong, China / Residing in Shenzhen, China > p. 177

yntala@126.com

Tala Yuan holds a BA in product design from South China Normal University, Guangzhou, as well as a BA and an MFA in gemstone and jewellery from the University of Applied Sciences Trier in Idar-Oberstein, Germany. She currently works as an assistant in Shenzhen Polytechnic's jewellery design department.

Tamara Grüner Pforzheim / Germany > p. 112

tamaragruener@gmx.de | www.schmuck-designerin.de

After her studies at the University of Applied Arts in Pforzheim in 2006, she started designing for the jewelry industry. Since 2014 she teaches at the Goldsmith' School in Pforzheim. Spontaneity and artificiality have a powerful dialogue in Tamara's works. This duality is the central theme of her actual body of work, called "Sahara". Shapes made with bones or synthetic materials contrast with angular minerals and metals. The single elements form an ensemble in which the lines become indistinct. An intense artificiality is produced by iridescent, rainbow-coloured surfaces: natural materials such as mother-of-pearl seem to possess unnatural qualities.

Tami Eshed Tel Aviv, Israel > p. 178-179

tamimamie@gmail.com | www.facebook.com/tsquared.tamieshed

In 2011, I graduated from a design programme at Shenkar College of Engineering and Design. My brand is called T Squared. The letter T represents my name, while Squared describes my approach to expression and to my designs, which are influenced by architecture, geometric lines, minimalism and monochromatic colours. I draw inspiration from urban architecture, which I take in through wandering the streets of my home city of Tel Aviv and observing its Bauhaus balconies and various unique structures. Environmental consciousness is something that I incorporate into my work because I see it as an integral part of our contemporary lives. We all try to minimize the use of harmful materials and recycle, and the world of jewellery design is no exception to this trend.

Tanel Veenre Tallinn, Estonia > p. 140-141

tanel.veenre@gmail.com | www.tanelveenre.com

The Estonian Academy of Arts and the Gerrit Rietveld Akademie in Amsterdam are where Tanel Veenre received his jewellery education. He has shown his work at over two hundred exhibitions and events. Although he is active in the art jewellery field, half of his heart also belongs to his fashion jewellery brand Tanel Veenre Jewellery. Tanel's pieces are all about communication and personal connections: "We all come to this world alone and leave it in solitude, but during the time given to us we try to find friends, kindred spirits and love," he says. "Jewellery is my way to talk with my people."

Tara Locklear Fayetteville, NC, USA / Residing in Raleigh, NC, USA > p. 124-125

locklleartara@gmail.com | taralocklear.com

Inspired by urban landscapes, Tara Locklear's designs comprise industrial and repurposed materials, which she uses to create a visual conversation in the form of jewellery. Her affinity for colour and bold shapes is a reflection of years of her receiving pop culture influences. Her work can be found at galleries such as Mora Contemporary Jewelry, NC, and Velvet da Vinci, CA, at the Smithsonian and American Craft Council Craft Shows, and in public collections including that of the Racine Art Museum, WI. She has recently been featured in American Craft Magazine and has participated in exhibitions nationally and in Canada. She is a current and active member of the Society of North American Goldsmiths and sits on its nominations and elections committee.

Theo Fennell London, UK > p. 50, 64-65

www.theofennell.com

Theo Fennell went to Eton in the 1960s and became the first pupil there in living memory to go to art college. He formed a studio and workshop in Chelsea in the late 1970s, a period when the area was home to some of the most brilliant artists and craftsmen in the country. Theo takes pride in being involved with every phase of creation so that his vision is realized down to the last detail. His passion for invention, craftsmanship and originality remains the ethos of his business. The influence of travel, discovery and eclecticism is prevalent in his work. There is a story behind every piece, as he incorporates quirky, beautifully detailed design into classical and romantic tradition, making every piece distinctive and inspirational. He has numerous famous fans including Lady Gaga, Cara Delevingne, David Beckham and Sir Elton John.

Theo Smeets Valkenburg aan de Geul, The Netherlands / Residing in Wattenheim, Germany > p. 58-59, 98

post@theosmeets.com | www.theosmeets.com

The goal of my work is to create symbols of contemporary passion in the broadest sense of the word. Although I was trained as a traditional gold- and silversmith, I include in my jewellery any material that I like and find suitable for the particular piece. After completing my artistic training at Gerrit Rietveld Academy in Amsterdam, I set up my own studio in 1992. Since 1998, I have taught in Idar-Oberstein.

Tithi Kutchamuch Chiang Rai, Thailand / Residing in Bangkok, Thailand > p. 27

info@tithi.info | www.tithi.info

Tithi Kutchamuch received a bachelor's degree in architecture and industrial design from KMITL in Bangkok. She then studied at the Royal College of Art, London, where in 2005 she was awarded an MA. She is the recipient of numerous awards, including a best newcomer prize from Craft Council UK and a Deutsche Bank Award. She was also selected by Silpakorn University as Designer of the Year in both its jewellery and product categories, and she has been given several other accolades. Tithi's unconventional conceptual approach has led her to design a variety of interesting pieces that cross boundaries between decorative objects, functional jewellery, product design and architectural projects.

Tomoyo Hiraiwa Kanagawa Prefecture, Japan > p. 39
tomoyo-hiraiwa@ksh.biglobe.ne.jp | tomoyohiraiwa.com
When I select materials for my pieces, I focus on their simple beauty and the possibilities that they offer. My current thematic interest is classical Japanese culture, aesthetics and language. In particular, I am drawn to the native Japanese words known as Yamato Kotoba, which is the real Japanese language from a time when there wasn't so much outside language influence. Within this lexicon, beautiful, sophisticated words resonate in my mind, such as words that represent time, nature and the seasons. I also have an affinity with shapes and sounds that feel natural.

Tore Svensson Alfta, Sweden / Residing in Gothenburg, Sweden > p. 60
tore.s@comhem.se | www.toresvensson.com
Tore Svensson graduated in 1978 from the HDK School of Design and Craft in Gothenburg. Between 1989 and 1996, he taught at HDK and later served as a professor in its jewellery department. His work includes jewellery and objects and is presented in private and public collections as well as in museums all over the world. He is a recipient of several awards, including the Hermann Hoffmann Prize. Tore principally works with steel, the surface of which he attempts to alter through different techniques such as etching, gilding and painting. He only incorporates shapes that he considers necessary and are inspired by his surroundings into his work.

Tove Knuts Leksand, Sweden / Residing in Stockholm, Sweden > p. 73
info@toveknuts.se | www. toveknuts.se
Tove Knuts graduated from the University College of Arts, Crafts and Design in Konstfack, Sweden. She participated in the fifth Tallinn Applied Art Triennial in Estonia in 2005, the 2010 edition of Minimum, the 2015 edition of Boundaries and the 2016 edition of City (where she won the grand prize for her work) at the International Jewellery Festival in Legnica, Poland. She's been showcased at the Röhsska Design Museum in Gothenburg, Malmö Konsthall and Gustavsbergs Konsthall. She has had two solo exhibitions in Stockholm, Sweden (in 2012 at Daughters and in 2015 at Gallery Movitz). In 2017, she became a member of Nutida Svenskt Silver, a contemporary gallery in Stockholm.

Tsang-Hsuan Lin Hsihchu, Taiwan / Residing in Taichung, Taiwan > p. 61
linusqlin@gmail.com | linusqlin28.wixsite.com/tsanghsuanlin
Although I initially majored in electronics, at college I decided to focus on metalsmithing and contemporary jewellery. I study metalsmithing at TNNUA, where I am pursuing a master's degree. I also studied at Sydney College of Arts as a postgraduate exchange student. In my work, I attempt to reexamine the value of precious things through electronic materials that are available almost everywhere but go unnoticed or are given little attention.

Tyler Stoll Roanoke, VA, Richmond, VA > p. 25
tylercstoll@gmail.com | www.tylerstoll.com
Tyler Stoll received his craft education from community art centres and craft schools around the United States. He recently completed the Core Fellowship at Penland School of Crafts, a two-year emerging-artist programme in the mountains of North Carolina. Tyler currently lives, works and teaches in Richmond, VA. My current body of work developed out of an attempt to release frustration with and eventually express gratitude for parts of my body with which I feels at odds. Arranging and reimagining these shapes out of context makes them appear simultaneously comforting and disconcerting, familiar and alien. It is my hope that, once worn, these pieces take on a humorous life of their own.

>> U >>

Una Mikuda Latvia > p. 43, 223
una.mikuda@gmail.com | www.unamikuda.com
I am a graduate of the bachelor's programme at the Art Academy of Latvia, and I am working towards completing a master's programme as I seek to perfect my personal style and master various metal-processing technologies. I believe that art enriches the world; it impacts the environment and people in it, including me I relish the task of producing one-off pieces: each piece I make, I consider to be unique, and each of them should have a well-considered technical performance plan. Therefore, every piece of jewellery is like a new challenge for me.

Ute Decker Germany / Residing in London, UK > p. 171
www.utedecker.com
Ute Decker is best known for her minimalist jewellery art. This self-taught designer has created an innovative method of sculpting, bending and twisting gold and silver into expressive three-dimensional geometric poetry. The clean lines of her pieces reflect the purity of her materials' provenance. As a political economist-turned-journalist-turned-artist jeweller, Ute Decker is a pioneer of the international ethical jewellery movement and one of the first worldwide to work with Fairtrade Gold. Her unique and limited edition sculptures are engaging when worn on the body as they are when displayed on a plinth. Her work has been exhibited internationally, and it can be found in notable private and public collections including that of the Victoria & Albert Museum.

>> V >>

Veroniek Dutré Sint-Niklaas, Belgium > p. 174
veronika_dutre@yahoo.com | www.veronika-art.blogspot.be
Veroniek Dutré obtained a Ph.D. in chemical engineering at the University of Leuven, Belgium, before becoming fascinated by jewellery design. She has followed many jewellery-related courses over the past fifteen years, and she is continuously challenging herself with new techniques; for example, she recently finished her training in gemstone-setting techniques. Veroniek's work is recognizable through its minimalistic, geometric and abstract forms. She gets her inspiration from her engineering background, architecture and nature, which she translates into its purest forms.

>> W >>

WALKA (Claudia Betancourt and Nano Pulgar) Santiago de Chile > p. 137
info@walka.cl | www.walka.cl
WALKA is a contemporary jewellery studio based in Chile. Claudia Betancourt and Nano Pulgar established the studio in 2004. They both entered the jewellery world as a result of their backgrounds as third-generation members of traditional Chilean craft families. They work on cultural identity, collaboration, relations between globalization and local visual identity, and art-craft-design relations. Their pieces have been exhibited in museums and galleries and at events in the United States, Finland; Chile and Spain, and they have a constant presence in fashion publications such as Vogue, Harper's Bazaar and Elle, among others. They also run the WE WALKA School of Jewellery, one of the most significant hubs of jewellery studies in Latin America.

Wendy McAllister Baltimore, MD > p. 113, 221
www.wendymcallister.com
Wendy McAllister's sculptural enamelled brooches have been exhibited internationally at galleries, museums and art fairs, including Klimt02 Gallery (Barcelona, Spain), Charon Kransen Arts at SOFA Chicago Art Fair, SIERAAD Jewellery Art Fair (Amsterdam), Shanghai Jewellery Design Centre and the Mint Museum of Craft and Design (Charlotte, NC). She received a BFA in Ceramics from George Washington University and a post baccalaureate certificate in jewellery from the Maryland Institute College of Art. Nature is where Wendy finds her inspiration: "In the natural world, the vibrant exuberance of enticing and often forbidding forms, all with an endless array of textures, clashing colours and underlying geometry, excites me even as I struggle to accept its impermanence."

William Rudolph Faulkner San Jose, CA, USA / Residing in Berlin, Germany > p. 208
rudolphsemail@gmail.com | www.WilliamRudolphFaulkner.com
William received a BFA in sculpture from San Jose State University before receiving an MFA in studio glass from Southern Illinois University Carbondale in 2013. He moved to Germany and continued his education at the Hochschule Trier in Idar-Oberstein, where he received another master's, this time in in gemstone and jewellery design, in 2016. He is now living and working in Berlin as a gaffer and instructor at Berlin Glas and as a freelance artist. His current work is a reflection of the social situations that a group of people encounters when interacting with other groups of people who have different ideologies. The pieces are recreations of objects that separate groups of people who can no longer communicate while living in close proximity to each other.

>> X >>

Xenia Walschikow Nytwa, Russia / Residing in Birmingham, UK > p. 121
mail@xeniawalschikow.com | www.xeniawalschikow.com
Xenia was born in Russia and raised in Germany, and she now lives in Britain. She decided to leave behind a career in international business and retrain in the field of jewellery design. She has recently completed her master's at the Birmingham City University in England and is now creating wearable acrylic paint jewellery. Her inspiration comes from khokhloma, a traditional Russian decorative art. The aim of her work is to extract the detail of brush strokes and transform them into wearable art jewellery.

>> Y >>

Yi-Jen Chu Taiwan / Residing in Birmingham, UK > p. 89
chuyijen19922@gmail.com | chuyijen199221.wix.com/sandy
In 2016, Yi-Jen Chu graduated from the jewellery, silversmithing and related products master's programme at Birmingham City University. Chu's work explores the scattering and movement of water from mechanized systems such as taps and washing machines. Chu finds enjoyment in the movement of objects and their interaction with the body and explores this theme through creating objects that rotate, open, close and shut as the body moves.

Yiota Vogli Athens, Greece > p. 18, 153
vogliyiota@gmail.com | www.yiotavogli.com
Yiota Vogli is the coauthor of two books on jewellery that were published by the Greek Ministry of Education. Her works have been shown at numerous exhibitions in Greece and abroad. As a visual artist, her relationship with jewellery is bidirectional, and her work as a jeweller is influenced by her artistic research. Based on the premise that observation and painting require the engagement of all of our senses, in her work she draws on memory and therefore on her senses. By approaching jewellery as a form of microsculpture, she refers to form, material, colours and texture to conceptualize personal memories and her view of social and cultural issues and then turn them into art.

Yiqing Cai Shanghai, China / Residing in Düsseldorf, Germany > p. 111
info@yiqingcai.com | www.yiqingcai.com
The focus of Yiqing Cai's work is the organs found in the human body, because of the essential role that they play and our dependence on them. She is interested in their parallels with plant structures, which often have similar properties and ultimately follow the same goal. For example, she has created pieces that reveal the similarities between the structure of the human lungs and the roots of growing plant embryos.

Yojae Lee Seoul, South Korea > p. 12-13
leeyojae@naver.com | www.leeyojae.com
Each of my insect pieces follows a similar formula: a body consisting of six legs, two feelers and skin. They express the discomfort that may result from their being overly specific and explicit through the use of exaggerated size and unique texture. The result is not only shocking but also intensely powerful and, arguably, surreal. People see what they want to see. It is possible that my work could cause discomfort among some viewers and fascination among others. Regardless, it is up to them to decide.

Younha Jung Busan, South Korea / Residing in the United States > p. 87
younha.metal@gmail.com | younhajung.com
Younha's work expresses the emotional shifts that humans feel as they adapt to change in their surroundings. Currently, she is making jewellery from repurposed steel and found objects. These materials represent the environment in which they were found, and the artwork that she creates with them expresses the point of view of an insider or outsider regarding a particular point in time. Her work is both site-specific and universal, because the materials that she uses are commonplace and familiar.

Yvonne Gilhooly Edinburgh, Scotland, UK / Residing in Gourock, Scotland, UK > p. 37
yvonnegilhooly@yahoo.co.uk | www.yvonnegilhooly.co.uk
Deploying traditional goldsmithing skills, Yvonne's practice is an exploration of geometry in all its poetic forms. Her fascination with line, form, volume and the void is where she begins. Process is key, as her designs continue to develop whilst at the bench, allowing Yvonne to respond intuitively to materials. Her recent work showcases a bold combination of gemstones and precious metals in an exploration of shadow and light. Ultimately, Yvonne's aim is to create covetable, thought-provoking jewellery.